_____

_____

_____

"Traveling leaves you speechless,

then turns you into a storyteller."

- Ibn Battuta

Date: _____	From: _____	Beginning Mileage: _____
Weather:	To: _____	Ending Mileage: _____
	Route Taken: _____	
	_____	Total Miles Traveled: _____

Campground Information

Name: _____

Address: _____

Phone: _____

Site # _____ $_____ ☐ Day ☐ Week ☐ Month

☐ First Visit   ☐ Return Visit   ☐ Easy Access
☐ Site Level   ☐ Back-in   ☐ Pull-through
☐ 15 amp   ☐ 30 amp   ☐ 50 amp
☐ Water   ☐ Sewer   ☐ Shade ☐ Sun
☐ Paved   ☐ Sand / Grass   ☐ Gravel
☐ Picnic Table   ☐ Fire ring   ☐ Trees ☐ Lawn
☐ Patio   ☐ Kid Friendly   ☐ Pet Friendly
☐ Store   ☐ Cafe   ☐ Firewood
☐ Ice   ☐ Security   ☐ Quiet ☐ Noisy

Our Rating: ☆ ☆ ☆ ☆ ☆

GPS: _____

Altitude: _____

Cell Service / Carrier: _____

☐ Antenna Reception   ☐ Satellite TV   ☐ Cable TV
☐ Wifi Available   ☐ Free ☐ Fee $_____

Memberships: _____

Ammenities: _____

Location	☺	😐	☹	Water Pressure	☺	😐	☹
Restrooms	☺	😐	☹	Laundry	☺	😐	☹
Pool	☺	😐	☹	Hot Tub	☺	😐	☹

Places Visited / Activities:

_____
_____
_____
_____

People Met / New Friends:

_____
_____
_____
_____

Food, Dining & Restaurants:

_____
_____
_____
_____

Highlights / Memorable Events:

_____
_____
_____
_____

Places To Go & Things To Do for Next Time:

_____
_____
_____
_____

NOTES:

Date: _____

Weather:

☀ ☁ ☂ ❄

🌡 🌡 🚩 ☁

From: _____

To: _____

Route Taken: _____

_____

Beginning Mileage: _____

Ending Mileage: _____

Total Miles Traveled: _____

CAMPGROUND INFORMATION

Name: _____

Address: _____

Phone: _____

Site #_____ $_____ ☐ Day ☐ Week ☐ Month

☐ First Visit   ☐ Return Visit   ☐ Easy Access
☐ Site Level   ☐ Back-in   ☐ Pull-through
☐ 15 amp   ☐ 30 amp   ☐ 50 amp
☐ Water   ☐ Sewer   ☐ Shade ☐ Sun
☐ Paved   ☐ Sand / Grass   ☐ Gravel
☐ Picnic Table   ☐ Fire ring   ☐ Trees ☐ Lawn
☐ Patio   ☐ Kid Friendly   ☐ Pet Friendly
☐ Store   ☐ Cafe   ☐ Firewood
☐ Ice   ☐ Security   ☐ Quiet ☐ Noisy

Our Rating: ☆ ☆ ☆ ☆ ☆

GPS: _____

Altitude: _____

Cell Service / Carrier: _____

☐ Antenna Reception   ☐ Satellite TV   ☐ Cable TV
☐ Wifi Available   ☐ Free ☐ Fee $_____

Memberships: _____

Ammenities: _____

Location	☺	☺	☹	Water Pressure	☺	☺ ☹
Restrooms	☺	☺	☹	Laundry	☺	☺ ☹
Pool	☺	☺	☹	Hot Tub	☺	☺ ☹

PLACES VISITED / ACTIVITIES:

_____

_____

_____

PEOPLE MET / NEW FRIENDS:

_____

_____

_____

FOOD, DINING & RESTAURANTS:

_____

_____

_____

HIGHLIGHTS / MEMORABLE EVENTS:

_____

_____

_____

PLACES TO GO & THINGS TO DO FOR NEXT TIME:

_____

_____

_____

_____

NOTES:

Date: _____	From: _____	Beginning Mileage: _____
Weather:	To: _____	Ending Mileage: _____
☀ ☁ ☂ ❄ 🌡 ❄🌡 📢 ☁	Route Taken: _____ _____	Total Miles Traveled: _____

CAMPGROUND INFORMATION

Name:_____ | Our Rating: ☆ ☆ ☆ ☆ ☆

Address:_____ | GPS: _____

Phone:_____ | Altitude: _____

Site #_____ $_____ ☐ Day ☐ Week ☐ Month | Cell Service / Carrier: _____

☐ First Visit	☐ Return Visit	☐ Easy Access
☐ Site Level	☐ Back-in	☐ Pull-through
☐ 15 amp	☐ 30 amp	☐ 50 amp
☐ Water	☐ Sewer	☐ Shade ☐ Sun
☐ Paved	☐ Sand / Grass	☐ Gravel
☐ Picnic Table	☐ Fire ring	☐ Trees ☐ Lawn
☐ Patio	☐ Kid Friendly	☐ Pet Friendly
☐ Store	☐ Cafe	☐ Firewood
☐ Ice	☐ Security	☐ Quiet ☐ Noisy

☐ Antenna Reception ☐ Satellite TV ☐ Cable TV
☐ Wifi Available ☐ Free ☐ Fee $_____

Memberships: _____
Ammenities:_____

Location	☺ ☺ ☹	Water Pressure	☺ ☺ ☹
Restrooms	☺ ☺ ☹	Laundry	☺ ☺ ☹
Pool	☺ ☺ ☹	Hot Tub	☺ ☺ ☹

PLACES VISITED / ACTIVITIES:
_____
_____
_____
_____

PEOPLE MET / NEW FRIENDS:
_____
_____
_____
_____

FOOD, DINING & RESTAURANTS:
_____
_____
_____
_____

HIGHLIGHTS / MEMORABLE EVENTS:
_____
_____
_____
_____

PLACES TO GO & THINGS TO DO FOR NEXT TIME:
_____
_____
_____
_____

NOTES:

Date: _____	From: _____	Beginning Mileage:
Weather: ☀ ⛅ ☔ ❄ 🌡 🌡 🎐 💨	To: _____ Route Taken: _____ _____	Ending Mileage: _____ Total Miles Traveled:

CAMPGROUND INFORMATION

Name: _____	Our Rating: ☆ ☆ ☆ ☆ ☆
Address: _____	GPS: _____
Phone: _____	Altitude: _____

Site # _____ $ _____		☐ Day ☐ Week ☐ Month	Cell Service / Carrier: _____

☐ First Visit	☐ Return Visit	☐ Easy Access
☐ Site Level	☐ Back-in	☐ Pull-through
☐ 15 amp	☐ 30 amp	☐ 50 amp
☐ Water	☐ Sewer	☐ Shade ☐ Sun
☐ Paved	☐ Sand / Grass	☐ Gravel
☐ Picnic Table	☐ Fire ring	☐ Trees ☐ Lawn
☐ Patio	☐ Kid Friendly	☐ Pet Friendly
☐ Store	☐ Cafe	☐ Firewood
☐ Ice	☐ Security	☐ Quiet ☐ Noisy

☐ Antenna Reception ☐ Satellite TV ☐ Cable TV
☐ Wifi Available ☐ Free ☐ Fee $_____

Memberships: _____

Ammenities: _____

Location	☺ ☺ ☹	Water Pressure	☺ ☺ ☹
Restrooms	☺ ☺ ☹	Laundry	☺ ☺ ☹
Pool	☺ ☺ ☹	Hot Tub	☺ ☺ ☹

PLACES VISITED / ACTIVITIES: _____

_____
_____
_____

PEOPLE MET / NEW FRIENDS: _____

_____
_____
_____

FOOD, DINING & RESTAURANTS: _____

_____
_____
_____

HIGHLIGHTS / MEMORABLE EVENTS: _____

_____
_____
_____

PLACES TO GO & THINGS TO DO FOR NEXT TIME: _____

_____
_____
_____

NOTES:

Date: _____	From: _____	Beginning Mileage:
Weather:	To: _____	_____
☀ ⛅ ☔ ❄	Route Taken: _____	Ending Mileage:
🌡 🌡 🚩 🌩	_____	_____
		Total Miles Traveled:

Campground Information

Name:_____	Our Rating: ☆ ☆ ☆ ☆ ☆
Address:_____	GPS: _____
Phone:_____	Altitude: _____

| Site #_____ $_____ ☐ Day ☐ Week ☐ Month | Cell Service / Carrier:_____ |

☐ First Visit	☐ Return Visit	☐ Easy Access	☐ Antenna Reception	☐ Satellite TV	☐ Cable TV
☐ Site Level	☐ Back-in	☐ Pull-through	☐ Wifi Available	☐ Free ☐ Fee $_____
☐ 15 amp	☐ 30 amp	☐ 50 amp	Memberships: _____
☐ Water	☐ Sewer	☐ Shade ☐ Sun	Ammenities:_____
☐ Paved	☐ Sand / Grass	☐ Gravel	
☐ Picnic Table	☐ Fire ring	☐ Trees ☐ Lawn	

			☺ ☺ ☹		☺ ☺ ☹
☐ Patio	☐ Kid Friendly	☐ Pet Friendly	Location ☺ ☺ ☹	Water Pressure	☺ ☺ ☹
☐ Store	☐ Cafe	☐ Firewood	Restrooms ☺ ☺ ☹	Laundry	☺ ☺ ☹
☐ Ice	☐ Security	☐ Quiet ☐ Noisy	Pool ☺ ☺ ☹	Hot Tub	☺ ☺ ☹

Places Visited / Activities:
_____
_____
_____
_____

People Met / New Friends:
_____
_____
_____
_____

Food, Dining & Restaurants:
_____
_____
_____
_____

Highlights / Memorable Events:
_____
_____
_____
_____

Places To Go & Things To Do for Next Time:
_____
_____
_____
_____

NOTES:

Date: _____	From: _____	Beginning Mileage: _____
Weather: ☀ ⛅ ☂ ❄ 🌡 🌡 🚩 ☁	To: _____ Route Taken: _____ _____	Ending Mileage: _____ Total Miles Traveled: _____

CAMPGROUND INFORMATION

Name:_____

Address:_____

Phone:_____

Site #_____ $_____ ☐ Day ☐ Week ☐ Month

☐ First Visit	☐ Return Visit	☐ Easy Access
☐ Site Level	☐ Back-in	☐ Pull-through
☐ 15 amp	☐ 30 amp	☐ 50 amp
☐ Water	☐ Sewer	☐ Shade ☐ Sun
☐ Paved	☐ Sand / Grass	☐ Gravel
☐ Picnic Table	☐ Fire ring	☐ Trees ☐ Lawn
☐ Patio	☐ Kid Friendly	☐ Pet Friendly
☐ Store	☐ Cafe	☐ Firewood
☐ Ice	☐ Security	☐ Quiet ☐ Noisy

Our Rating: ☆ ☆ ☆ ☆ ☆

GPS: _____

Altitude: _____

Cell Service / Carrier:_____

☐ Antenna Reception   ☐ Satellite TV   ☐ Cable TV
☐ Wifi Available   ☐ Free ☐ Fee $_____

Memberships: _____

Ammenities:_____

Location	☺	☺	☹	Water Pressure	☺	☺	☹
Restrooms	☺	☺	☹	Laundry	☺	☺	☹
Pool	☺	☺	☹	Hot Tub	☺	☺	☹

PLACES VISITED / ACTIVITIES:
_____
_____
_____
_____

PEOPLE MET / NEW FRIENDS:
_____
_____
_____
_____

FOOD, DINING & RESTAURANTS:
_____
_____
_____
_____

HIGHLIGHTS / MEMORABLE EVENTS:
_____
_____
_____
_____

PLACES TO GO & THINGS TO DO FOR NEXT TIME:
_____
_____
_____
_____

NOTES:

Date: _____	From: _____	Beginning Mileage:
Weather:	To: _____	_____
☀ ⛅ ☔ ❄	Route Taken: _____	Ending Mileage:
🌡 🌡 🎏 ☁	_____	_____
		Total Miles Traveled:

CAMPGROUND INFORMATION

Name: _____   Our Rating: ☆ ☆ ☆ ☆ ☆

Address: _____   GPS: _____

Phone: _____   Altitude: _____

Site # _____ $ _____ ☐ Day ☐ Week ☐ Month   Cell Service / Carrier: _____

☐ First Visit ☐ Return Visit ☐ Easy Access

☐ Antenna Reception ☐ Satellite TV ☐ Cable TV

☐ Site Level ☐ Back-in ☐ Pull-through   ☐ Wifi Available ☐ Free ☐ Fee $ _____

☐ 15 amp ☐ 30 amp ☐ 50 amp

☐ Water ☐ Sewer ☐ Shade ☐ Sun   Memberships: _____

☐ Paved ☐ Sand / Grass ☐ Gravel   Ammenities: _____

☐ Picnic Table ☐ Fire ring ☐ Trees ☐ Lawn

Location	☺ ☺ ☹		Water Pressure	☺ ☺ ☹		
Restrooms	☺ ☺ ☹		Laundry	☺ ☺ ☹		
Pool	☺ ☺ ☹		Hot Tub	☺ ☺ ☹		

☐ Patio ☐ Kid Friendly ☐ Pet Friendly

☐ Store ☐ Cafe ☐ Firewood

☐ Ice ☐ Security ☐ Quiet ☐ Noisy

PLACES VISITED / ACTIVITIES: _____

_____

_____

_____

PEOPLE MET / NEW FRIENDS: _____

_____

_____

_____

FOOD, DINING & RESTAURANTS: _____

_____

_____

_____

HIGHLIGHTS / MEMORABLE EVENTS: _____

_____

_____

_____

PLACES TO GO & THINGS TO DO FOR NEXT TIME: _____

_____

_____

_____

_____

NOTES:

Date: _____

Weather:
☀ ⛅ ☔ ❄
🌡 🌡 📢 🌩

From: _____

To: _____

Route Taken: _____

_____

Beginning Mileage:
_____

Ending Mileage:
_____

Total Miles Traveled:
_____

CAMPGROUND INFORMATION

Name: _____

Address: _____

Phone: _____

Our Rating: ☆ ☆ ☆ ☆ ☆

GPS: _____

Altitude: _____

Cell Service / Carrier: _____

Site # _____ $ _____ ☐ Day ☐ Week ☐ Month

☐ First Visit	☐ Return Visit	☐ Easy Access
☐ Site Level	☐ Back-in	☐ Pull-through
☐ 15 amp	☐ 30 amp	☐ 50 amp
☐ Water	☐ Sewer	☐ Shade ☐ Sun
☐ Paved	☐ Sand / Grass	☐ Gravel
☐ Picnic Table	☐ Fire ring	☐ Trees ☐ Lawn
☐ Patio	☐ Kid Friendly	☐ Pet Friendly
☐ Store	☐ Cafe	☐ Firewood
☐ Ice	☐ Security	☐ Quiet ☐ Noisy

☐ Antenna Reception   ☐ Satellite TV   ☐ Cable TV
☐ Wifi Available   ☐ Free ☐ Fee $ _____

Memberships: _____

Ammenities: _____

Location	☺ ☺ ☹	Water Pressure	☺ ☺ ☹
Restrooms	☺ ☺ ☹	Laundry	☺ ☺ ☹
Pool	☺ ☺ ☹	Hot Tub	☺ ☺ ☹

PLACES VISITED / ACTIVITIES: _____

_____

_____

_____

PEOPLE MET / NEW FRIENDS: _____

_____

_____

_____

FOOD, DINING & RESTAURANTS: _____

_____

_____

_____

HIGHLIGHTS / MEMORABLE EVENTS: _____

_____

_____

_____

PLACES TO GO & THINGS TO DO FOR NEXT TIME: _____

_____

_____

_____

NOTES:

Date: _____	From: _____	Beginning Mileage: _____
Weather:	To: _____	Ending Mileage: _____
☀ ⛅ ☔ ❄ 🌡 🌡 🎏 ☁	Route Taken: _____ _____	Total Miles Traveled:

Campground Information

Name:_____

Address:_____

Phone:_____

Site #_____ $_____ ☐ Day ☐ Week ☐ Month

☐ First Visit	☐ Return Visit	☐ Easy Access
☐ Site Level	☐ Back-in	☐ Pull-through
☐ 15 amp	☐ 30 amp	☐ 50 amp
☐ Water	☐ Sewer	☐ Shade ☐ Sun
☐ Paved	☐ Sand / Grass	☐ Gravel
☐ Picnic Table	☐ Fire ring	☐ Trees ☐ Lawn
☐ Patio	☐ Kid Friendly	☐ Pet Friendly
☐ Store	☐ Cafe	☐ Firewood
☐ Ice	☐ Security	☐ Quiet ☐ Noisy

Our Rating: ☆ ☆ ☆ ☆ ☆

GPS: _____

Altitude: _____

Cell Service / Carrier:_____

☐ Antenna Reception ☐ Satellite TV ☐ Cable TV
☐ Wifi Available ☐ Free ☐ Fee $_____

Memberships: _____

Ammenities:_____

	☺ ☺ ☹		☺ ☺ ☹
Location	☺ 😐 ☹	Water Pressure	☺ 😐 ☹
Restrooms	☺ 😐 ☹	Laundry	☺ 😐 ☹
Pool	☺ 😐 ☹	Hot Tub	☺ 😐 ☹

Places Visited / Activities: _____
_____
_____
_____

People Met / New Friends: _____
_____
_____
_____

Food, Dining & Restaurants: _____
_____
_____
_____

Highlights / Memorable Events: _____
_____
_____
_____

Places To Go & Things To Do for Next Time: _____
_____
_____
_____

NOTES:

Date: _____	From: _____	Beginning Mileage: _____
Weather:	To: _____	Ending Mileage: _____
☀ ⛅ ☔ ❄	Route Taken: _____	
🌡 🌡 🎐 🌳	_____	Total Miles Traveled: _____

CAMPGROUND INFORMATION

Name:_____	Our Rating: ☆ ☆ ☆ ☆ ☆
Address:_____	GPS: _____
Phone:_____	Altitude: _____

Site #_____ $_____ ☐ Day ☐ Week ☐ Month

| | | | Cell Service / Carrier:_____ |

☐ First Visit   ☐ Return Visit   ☐ Easy Access
☐ Site Level   ☐ Back-in   ☐ Pull-through
☐ 15 amp   ☐ 30 amp   ☐ 50 amp
☐ Water   ☐ Sewer   ☐ Shade   ☐ Sun
☐ Paved   ☐ Sand / Grass   ☐ Gravel
☐ Picnic Table   ☐ Fire ring   ☐ Trees   ☐ Lawn
☐ Patio   ☐ Kid Friendly   ☐ Pet Friendly
☐ Store   ☐ Cafe   ☐ Firewood
☐ Ice   ☐ Security   ☐ Quiet   ☐ Noisy

☐ Antenna Reception   ☐ Satellite TV   ☐ Cable TV
☐ Wifi Available   ☐ Free ☐ Fee $_____

Memberships: _____

Amenities:_____

Location	☺	☻	☹	Water Pressure	☺	☻	☹
Restrooms	☺	☻	☹	Laundry	☺	☻	☹
Pool	☺	☻	☹	Hot Tub	☺	☻	☹

PLACES VISITED / ACTIVITIES: _____

_____
_____
_____

PEOPLE MET / NEW FRIENDS: _____

_____
_____
_____

FOOD, DINING & RESTAURANTS: _____

_____
_____
_____

HIGHLIGHTS / MEMORABLE EVENTS: _____

_____
_____
_____

PLACES TO GO & THINGS TO DO FOR NEXT TIME: _____

_____
_____
_____

NOTES:

Date: _____	From: _____	Beginning Mileage: _____
Weather: ☀ ⛅ ☔ ❄ 🌡 🌡 🎐 ☁	To: _____ Route Taken: _____ _____	Ending Mileage: _____ Total Miles Traveled: _____

CAMPGROUND INFORMATION

Name: _____

Address: _____

Phone: _____

Site # _____ $ _____ ☐ Day ☐ Week ☐ Month

☐ First Visit	☐ Return Visit	☐ Easy Access
☐ Site Level	☐ Back-in	☐ Pull-through
☐ 15 amp	☐ 30 amp	☐ 50 amp
☐ Water	☐ Sewer	☐ Shade ☐ Sun
☐ Paved	☐ Sand / Grass	☐ Gravel
☐ Picnic Table	☐ Fire ring	☐ Trees ☐ Lawn
☐ Patio	☐ Kid Friendly	☐ Pet Friendly
☐ Store	☐ Cafe	☐ Firewood
☐ Ice	☐ Security	☐ Quiet ☐ Noisy

Our Rating: ☆ ☆ ☆ ☆ ☆

GPS: _____

Altitude: _____

Cell Service / Carrier: _____

☐ Antenna Reception ☐ Satellite TV ☐ Cable TV
☐ Wifi Available ☐ Free ☐ Fee $_____

Memberships: _____

Ammenities: _____

	☺	☺	☹		☺	☺	☹
Location	☺	☺	☹	Water Pressure	☺	☺	☹
Restrooms	☺	☺	☹	Laundry	☺	☺	☹
Pool	☺	☺	☹	Hot Tub	☺	☺	☹

PLACES VISITED / ACTIVITIES: _____
_____
_____
_____

PEOPLE MET / NEW FRIENDS: _____
_____
_____
_____

FOOD, DINING & RESTAURANTS: _____
_____
_____
_____

HIGHLIGHTS / MEMORABLE EVENTS: _____
_____
_____
_____

PLACES TO GO & THINGS TO DO FOR NEXT TIME: _____
_____
_____
_____

NOTES:

Date: _____	From: _____	Beginning Mileage:
Weather:	To: _____	Ending Mileage:
☀ ☁ ☂ ❄	Route Taken: _____	
🌡 🌡 🎐 ☁	_____	Total Miles Traveled:

CAMPGROUND INFORMATION

Name:_____ Our Rating: ☆ ☆ ☆ ☆ ☆

Address:_____ GPS: _____

Phone:_____ Altitude: _____

Site #_____ $_____ ☐ Day ☐ Week ☐ Month | Cell Service / Carrier: _____

☐ First Visit	☐ Return Visit	☐ Easy Access	
☐ Site Level	☐ Back-in	☐ Pull-through	
☐ 15 amp	☐ 30 amp	☐ 50 amp	
☐ Water	☐ Sewer	☐ Shade ☐ Sun	
☐ Paved	☐ Sand / Grass	☐ Gravel	
☐ Picnic Table	☐ Fire ring	☐ Trees ☐ Lawn	
☐ Patio	☐ Kid Friendly	☐ Pet Friendly	
☐ Store	☐ Cafe	☐ Firewood	
☐ Ice	☐ Security	☐ Quiet ☐ Noisy	

☐ Antenna Reception ☐ Satellite TV ☐ Cable TV
☐ Wifi Available ☐ Free ☐ Fee $_____

Memberships: _____

Ammenities:_____

Location	☺	☺	☹	Water Pressure	☺	☺	☹
Restrooms	☺	☺	☹	Laundry	☺	☺	☹
Pool	☺	☺	☹	Hot Tub	☺	☺	☹

PLACES VISITED / ACTIVITIES: _____
_____
_____
_____

PEOPLE MET / NEW FRIENDS: _____
_____
_____
_____

FOOD, DINING & RESTAURANTS: _____
_____
_____
_____

HIGHLIGHTS / MEMORABLE EVENTS: _____
_____
_____
_____

PLACES TO GO & THINGS TO DO FOR NEXT TIME: _____
_____
_____
_____

NOTES:

Date: _____	From: _____	Beginning Mileage:
Weather:	To: _____	_____
	Route Taken: _____	Ending Mileage:
	_____	_____
		Total Miles Traveled:

CAMPGROUND INFORMATION

Name: _____ Our Rating: ☆ ☆ ☆ ☆ ☆

Address: _____ GPS: _____

Phone: _____ Altitude: _____

Site # _____ $ _____ ☐ Day ☐ Week ☐ Month   Cell Service / Carrier: _____

☐ First Visit   ☐ Return Visit   ☐ Easy Access
☐ Site Level   ☐ Back-in   ☐ Pull-through
☐ 15 amp   ☐ 30 amp   ☐ 50 amp
☐ Water   ☐ Sewer   ☐ Shade   ☐ Sun
☐ Paved   ☐ Sand / Grass   ☐ Gravel
☐ Picnic Table   ☐ Fire ring   ☐ Trees   ☐ Lawn
☐ Patio   ☐ Kid Friendly   ☐ Pet Friendly
☐ Store   ☐ Cafe   ☐ Firewood
☐ Ice   ☐ Security   ☐ Quiet   ☐ Noisy

☐ Antenna Reception   ☐ Satellite TV   ☐ Cable TV
☐ Wifi Available   ☐ Free ☐ Fee $ _____

Memberships: _____

Ammenities: _____

Location	☺ ☺ ☹	Water Pressure	☺ ☺ ☹
Restrooms	☺ ☺ ☹	Laundry	☺ ☺ ☹
Pool	☺ ☺ ☹	Hot Tub	☺ ☺ ☹

PLACES VISITED / ACTIVITIES: _____

_____
_____
_____

PEOPLE MET / NEW FRIENDS: _____

_____
_____
_____

FOOD, DINING & RESTAURANTS: _____

_____
_____
_____

HIGHLIGHTS / MEMORABLE EVENTS: _____

_____
_____
_____

PLACES TO GO & THINGS TO DO FOR NEXT TIME: _____

_____
_____
_____

NOTES:

Date: _____	From: _____	Beginning Mileage:
Weather:	To: _____	_____
☀ ⛅ ☂ ❄	Route Taken: _____	Ending Mileage:
🌡 🌡 🚩 🌩	_____	Total Miles Traveled:

CAMPGROUND INFORMATION

Name: _____ Our Rating: ☆ ☆ ☆ ☆ ☆

Address: _____ GPS: _____

Phone: _____ Altitude: _____

Site # _____ $ _____ ☐ Day ☐ Week ☐ Month   Cell Service / Carrier: _____

☐ First Visit	☐ Return Visit	☐ Easy Access	
☐ Site Level	☐ Back-in	☐ Pull-through	
☐ 15 amp	☐ 30 amp	☐ 50 amp	
☐ Water	☐ Sewer	☐ Shade ☐ Sun	
☐ Paved	☐ Sand / Grass	☐ Gravel	
☐ Picnic Table	☐ Fire ring	☐ Trees ☐ Lawn	
☐ Patio	☐ Kid Friendly	☐ Pet Friendly	
☐ Store	☐ Cafe	☐ Firewood	
☐ Ice	☐ Security	☐ Quiet ☐ Noisy	

☐ Antenna Reception   ☐ Satellite TV   ☐ Cable TV
☐ Wifi Available   ☐ Free   ☐ Fee $ _____

Memberships: _____

Ammenities: _____

Location	☺ ☹ ☹	Water Pressure	☺ ☹ ☹
Restrooms	☺ ☹ ☹	Laundry	☺ ☹ ☹
Pool	☺ ☹ ☹	Hot Tub	☺ ☹ ☹

PLACES VISITED / ACTIVITIES:

_____
_____
_____
_____

PEOPLE MET / NEW FRIENDS:

_____
_____
_____
_____

FOOD, DINING & RESTAURANTS:

_____
_____
_____
_____

HIGHLIGHTS / MEMORABLE EVENTS:

_____
_____
_____
_____

PLACES TO GO & THINGS TO DO FOR NEXT TIME:

_____
_____
_____
_____

NOTES:

Date: _____	From: _____	Beginning Mileage:
Weather:	To: _____	_____
☀ ☁ ☔ ❄	Route Taken: _____	Ending Mileage:
🌡 🌡 🚩 ☁	_____	Total Miles Traveled:

CAMPGROUND INFORMATION

Name:_____

Address:_____

Phone:_____

Our Rating: ☆ ☆ ☆ ☆ ☆

GPS: _____

Altitude: _____

Cell Service / Carrier:_____

Site #_____ $_____ ☐ Day ☐ Week ☐ Month

☐ First Visit ☐ Return Visit ☐ Easy Access
☐ Site Level ☐ Back-in ☐ Pull-through
☐ 15 amp ☐ 30 amp ☐ 50 amp
☐ Water ☐ Sewer ☐ Shade ☐ Sun
☐ Paved ☐ Sand / Grass ☐ Gravel
☐ Picnic Table ☐ Fire ring ☐ Trees ☐ Lawn
☐ Patio ☐ Kid Friendly ☐ Pet Friendly
☐ Store ☐ Cafe ☐ Firewood
☐ Ice ☐ Security ☐ Quiet ☐ Noisy

☐ Antenna Reception ☐ Satellite TV ☐ Cable TV
☐ Wifi Available ☐ Free ☐ Fee $_____

Memberships: _____

Ammenities:_____

Location	☺ ☹	Water Pressure	☺ ☹
Restrooms	☺ ☹	Laundry	☺ ☹
Pool	☺ ☹	Hot Tub	☺ ☹

PLACES VISITED / ACTIVITIES: _____

_____
_____
_____

PEOPLE MET / NEW FRIENDS: _____

_____
_____
_____

FOOD, DINING & RESTAURANTS: _____

_____
_____
_____

HIGHLIGHTS / MEMORABLE EVENTS: _____

_____
_____
_____

PLACES TO GO & THINGS TO DO FOR NEXT TIME: _____

_____
_____
_____

NOTES:

Date: _____	From: _____	Beginning Mileage: _____
Weather:	To: _____	Ending Mileage: _____
☀ ⛅ ☂ ❄ / 🌡 🌡 🔦 ☁	Route Taken: _____ _____	Total Miles Traveled: _____

CAMPGROUND INFORMATION

Name:_____	Our Rating: ☆ ☆ ☆ ☆ ☆
Address:_____	GPS: _____
Phone:_____	Altitude: _____
Site #_____ $_____ ☐ Day ☐ Week ☐ Month	Cell Service / Carrier: _____

☐ First Visit	☐ Return Visit	☐ Easy Access	☐ Antenna Reception	☐ Satellite TV	☐ Cable TV
☐ Site Level	☐ Back-in	☐ Pull-through	☐ Wifi Available	☐ Free ☐ Fee	$_____
☐ 15 amp	☐ 30 amp	☐ 50 amp			
☐ Water	☐ Sewer	☐ Shade ☐ Sun	Memberships: _____		
☐ Paved	☐ Sand / Grass	☐ Gravel	Ammenities:_____		
☐ Picnic Table	☐ Fire ring	☐ Trees ☐ Lawn			

☐ Patio	☐ Kid Friendly	☐ Pet Friendly	Location	☺ ☺ ☹	Water Pressure	☺ ☺ ☹
☐ Store	☐ Cafe	☐ Firewood	Restrooms	☺ ☺ ☹	Laundry	☺ ☺ ☹
☐ Ice	☐ Security	☐ Quiet ☐ Noisy	Pool	☺ ☺ ☹	Hot Tub	☺ ☺ ☹

PLACES VISITED / ACTIVITIES: _____

_____

_____

_____

PEOPLE MET / NEW FRIENDS: _____

_____

_____

_____

FOOD, DINING & RESTAURANTS: _____

_____

_____

_____

HIGHLIGHTS / MEMORABLE EVENTS: _____

_____

_____

_____

PLACES TO GO & THINGS TO DO FOR NEXT TIME: _____

_____

_____

_____

NOTES:

Date: _____	From: _____	Beginning Mileage:
Weather:	To: _____	Ending Mileage:
☀ ⛅ ☔ ❄ 🌡 🌡 🚩 ⛈	Route Taken: _____ _____	Total Miles Traveled:

CAMPGROUND INFORMATION

Name:_____	Our Rating: ☆ ☆ ☆ ☆ ☆
Address:_____	GPS: _____
Phone:_____	Altitude: _____

| Site #_____ $_____ ☐ Day ☐ Week ☐ Month | Cell Service / Carrier:_____ |

☐ First Visit	☐ Return Visit	☐ Easy Access	☐ Antenna Reception ☐ Satellite TV ☐ Cable TV
☐ Site Level	☐ Back-in	☐ Pull-through	☐ Wifi Available ☐ Free ☐ Fee $_____
☐ 15 amp	☐ 30 amp	☐ 50 amp	
☐ Water	☐ Sewer	☐ Shade ☐ Sun	Memberships: _____
☐ Paved	☐ Sand / Grass	☐ Gravel	Ammenities:_____
☐ Picnic Table	☐ Fire ring	☐ Trees ☐ Lawn	

Location	☺ ☺ ☹	Water Pressure	☺ ☺ ☹
Restrooms	☺ ☺ ☹	Laundry	☺ ☺ ☹
Pool	☺ ☺ ☹	Hot Tub	☺ ☺ ☹

☐ Patio ☐ Kid Friendly ☐ Pet Friendly
☐ Store ☐ Cafe ☐ Firewood
☐ Ice ☐ Security ☐ Quiet ☐ Noisy

PLACES VISITED / ACTIVITIES: _____

_____
_____
_____

PEOPLE MET / NEW FRIENDS: _____

_____
_____
_____

FOOD, DINING & RESTAURANTS: _____

_____
_____
_____

HIGHLIGHTS / MEMORABLE EVENTS: _____

_____
_____
_____

PLACES TO GO & THINGS TO DO FOR NEXT TIME: _____

_____
_____
_____

NOTES:

Date: _____	From: _____	Beginning Mileage:
Weather:	To: _____	_____
☀ ⛅ ☔ ❄	Route Taken: _____	Ending Mileage:
🌡 🌡 🚩 ☁	_____	_____
		Total Miles Traveled:

Campground Information

Name:_____

Address:_____

Phone:_____

Our Rating: ☆ ☆ ☆ ☆ ☆

GPS: _____

Altitude: _____

Site #_____ $_____ ☐ Day ☐ Week ☐ Month

Cell Service / Carrier: _____

☐ First Visit	☐ Return Visit	☐ Easy Access
☐ Site Level	☐ Back-in	☐ Pull-through
☐ 15 amp	☐ 30 amp	☐ 50 amp
☐ Water	☐ Sewer	☐ Shade ☐ Sun
☐ Paved	☐ Sand / Grass	☐ Gravel
☐ Picnic Table	☐ Fire ring	☐ Trees ☐ Lawn
☐ Patio	☐ Kid Friendly	☐ Pet Friendly
☐ Store	☐ Cafe	☐ Firewood
☐ Ice	☐ Security	☐ Quiet ☐ Noisy

☐ Antenna Reception   ☐ Satellite TV   ☐ Cable TV
☐ Wifi Available   ☐ Free   ☐ Fee $_____

Memberships: _____

Ammenities:_____

Location	☺ ☺ ☹	Water Pressure	☺ ☺ ☹
Restrooms	☺ ☺ ☹	Laundry	☺ ☺ ☹
Pool	☺ ☺ ☹	Hot Tub	☺ ☺ ☹

Places Visited / Activities:
_____
_____
_____

People Met / New Friends:
_____
_____
_____

Food, Dining & Restaurants:
_____
_____
_____

Highlights / Memorable Events:
_____
_____
_____

Places To Go & Things To Do for Next Time:
_____
_____
_____

NOTES:

Date: _____	From: _____	Beginning Mileage: _____
Weather: ☀ ☁ ☂ ❄ 🌡 🌡 📣 🌳	To: _____ Route Taken: _____ _____	Ending Mileage: _____ Total Miles Traveled: _____

CAMPGROUND INFORMATION

Name:_____	Our Rating: ☆ ☆ ☆ ☆ ☆
Address:_____	GPS: _____
Phone:_____	Altitude: _____

Site #_____ $_____ ☐ Day ☐ Week ☐ Month

Cell Service / Carrier: _____

☐ First Visit	☐ Return Visit	☐ Easy Access
☐ Site Level	☐ Back-in	☐ Pull-through
☐ 15 amp	☐ 30 amp	☐ 50 amp
☐ Water	☐ Sewer	☐ Shade ☐ Sun
☐ Paved	☐ Sand / Grass	☐ Gravel
☐ Picnic Table	☐ Fire ring	☐ Trees ☐ Lawn
☐ Patio	☐ Kid Friendly	☐ Pet Friendly
☐ Store	☐ Cafe	☐ Firewood
☐ Ice	☐ Security	☐ Quiet ☐ Noisy

☐ Antenna Reception ☐ Satellite TV ☐ Cable TV
☐ Wifi Available   ☐ Free ☐ Fee $_____

Memberships: _____
Ammenities:_____

Location	☺	😐	☹	Water Pressure	☺	😐	☹
Restrooms	☺	😐	☹	Laundry	☺	😐	☹
Pool	☺	😐	☹	Hot Tub	☺	😐	☹

PLACES VISITED / ACTIVITIES: _____

_____
_____
_____

PEOPLE MET / NEW FRIENDS: _____

_____
_____
_____

FOOD, DINING & RESTAURANTS: _____

_____
_____
_____

HIGHLIGHTS / MEMORABLE EVENTS: _____

_____
_____
_____

PLACES TO GO & THINGS TO DO FOR NEXT TIME: _____

_____
_____
_____
_____

NOTES:

Date: _____   From: _____   Beginning Mileage: _____

Weather: To: _____   Ending Mileage: _____

☀ ☁ ☂ ❄   Route Taken: _____

🌡 🌡 🚩 ☁   _____   Total Miles Traveled: _____

CAMPGROUND INFORMATION

Name:_____   Our Rating: ☆ ☆ ☆ ☆ ☆

Address:_____   GPS: _____

Phone:_____   Altitude: _____

Site #_____ $_____ ☐ Day ☐ Week ☐ Month   Cell Service / Carrier:_____

☐ First Visit	☐ Return Visit	☐ Easy Access	
☐ Site Level	☐ Back-in	☐ Pull-through	
☐ 15 amp	☐ 30 amp	☐ 50 amp	
☐ Water	☐ Sewer	☐ Shade ☐ Sun	
☐ Paved	☐ Sand / Grass	☐ Gravel	
☐ Picnic Table	☐ Fire ring	☐ Trees ☐ Lawn	
☐ Patio	☐ Kid Friendly	☐ Pet Friendly	
☐ Store	☐ Cafe	☐ Firewood	
☐ Ice	☐ Security	☐ Quiet ☐ Noisy	

☐ Antenna Reception ☐ Satellite TV ☐ Cable TV
☐ Wifi Available ☐ Free ☐ Fee $_____

Memberships: _____

Ammenities:_____

Location	☺	☻	☹	Water Pressure	☺	☻	☹
Restrooms	☺	☻	☹	Laundry	☺	☻	☹
Pool	☺	☻	☹	Hot Tub	☺	☻	☹

PLACES VISITED / ACTIVITIES:
_____
_____
_____

PEOPLE MET / NEW FRIENDS:
_____
_____
_____

FOOD, DINING & RESTAURANTS:
_____
_____
_____

HIGHLIGHTS / MEMORABLE EVENTS:
_____
_____
_____

PLACES TO GO & THINGS TO DO FOR NEXT TIME:
_____
_____
_____
_____

NOTES:

Date: _____	From: _____	Beginning Mileage:
	To: _____	Ending Mileage:
Weather:	Route Taken: _____	
☀ ⛅ ☔ ❄	_____	Total Miles Traveled:
🌡 🌡 🎐 ☁		

CAMPGROUND INFORMATION

Name: _____   Our Rating: ☆ ☆ ☆ ☆ ☆

Address: _____   GPS: _____

Phone: _____   Altitude: _____

Site # _____ $ _____ ☐ Day ☐ Week ☐ Month   Cell Service / Carrier: _____

☐ First Visit   ☐ Return Visit   ☐ Easy Access   ☐ Antenna Reception   ☐ Satellite TV   ☐ Cable TV
☐ Site Level   ☐ Back-in   ☐ Pull-through   ☐ Wifi Available   ☐ Free ☐ Fee $_____
☐ 15 amp   ☐ 30 amp   ☐ 50 amp
☐ Water   ☐ Sewer   ☐ Shade ☐ Sun   Memberships: _____
☐ Paved   ☐ Sand / Grass   ☐ Gravel   Ammenities: _____
☐ Picnic Table   ☐ Fire ring   ☐ Trees ☐ Lawn

Location	☺ ☺ ☹	Water Pressure	☺ ☺ ☹
Restrooms	☺ ☺ ☹	Laundry	☺ ☺ ☹
Pool	☺ ☺ ☹	Hot Tub	☺ ☺ ☹

☐ Patio   ☐ Kid Friendly   ☐ Pet Friendly
☐ Store   ☐ Cafe   ☐ Firewood
☐ Ice   ☐ Security   ☐ Quiet ☐ Noisy

PLACES VISITED / ACTIVITIES: _____

_____

_____

_____

PEOPLE MET / NEW FRIENDS: _____

_____

_____

_____

FOOD, DINING & RESTAURANTS: _____

_____

_____

_____

HIGHLIGHTS / MEMORABLE EVENTS: _____

_____

_____

_____

PLACES TO GO & THINGS TO DO FOR NEXT TIME: _____

_____

_____

_____

NOTES:

Date: _____

Weather:

☀ ⛅ ☂ ❄
🌡 🌡 🎐 ☁

From: _____

To: _____

Route Taken: _____
_____

Beginning Mileage: _____

Ending Mileage: _____

Total Miles Traveled: _____

CAMPGROUND INFORMATION

Name: _____

Address: _____

Phone: _____

Site # _____ $ _____ ☐ Day ☐ Week ☐ Month

☐ First Visit	☐ Return Visit	☐ Easy Access
☐ Site Level	☐ Back-in	☐ Pull-through
☐ 15 amp	☐ 30 amp	☐ 50 amp
☐ Water	☐ Sewer	☐ Shade ☐ Sun
☐ Paved	☐ Sand / Grass	☐ Gravel
☐ Picnic Table	☐ Fire ring	☐ Trees ☐ Lawn
☐ Patio	☐ Kid Friendly	☐ Pet Friendly
☐ Store	☐ Cafe	☐ Firewood
☐ Ice	☐ Security	☐ Quiet ☐ Noisy

Our Rating: ☆ ☆ ☆ ☆ ☆

GPS: _____

Altitude: _____

Cell Service / Carrier: _____

☐ Antenna Reception   ☐ Satellite TV   ☐ Cable TV
☐ Wifi Available   ☐ Free ☐ Fee $_____

Memberships: _____

Ammenities: _____

Location	☺	😐	☹	Water Pressure	☺	😐	☹
Restrooms	☺	😐	☹	Laundry	☺	😐	☹
Pool	☺	😐	☹	Hot Tub	☺	😐	☹

PLACES VISITED / ACTIVITIES:
_____
_____
_____
_____

PEOPLE MET / NEW FRIENDS:
_____
_____
_____
_____

FOOD, DINING & RESTAURANTS:
_____
_____
_____
_____

HIGHLIGHTS / MEMORABLE EVENTS:
_____
_____
_____
_____

PLACES TO GO & THINGS TO DO FOR NEXT TIME:
_____
_____
_____
_____

NOTES:

Date: _____	From: _____	Beginning Mileage:
Weather:	To: _____	
☀ ⛅ 🌧 ❄	Route Taken: _____	Ending Mileage:
🌡 🌡 🎐 🌩	_____	Total Miles Traveled:

CAMPGROUND INFORMATION

Name:_____	Our Rating: ☆ ☆ ☆ ☆ ☆
Address:_____	GPS: _____
Phone:_____	Altitude: _____

Site #_____ $_____ ☐ Day ☐ Week ☐ Month

			Cell Service / Carrier:_____
☐ First Visit	☐ Return Visit	☐ Easy Access	
☐ Site Level	☐ Back-in	☐ Pull-through	☐ Antenna Reception ☐ Satellite TV ☐ Cable TV
☐ 15 amp	☐ 30 amp	☐ 50 amp	☐ Wifi Available ☐ Free ☐ Fee $_____
☐ Water	☐ Sewer	☐ Shade ☐ Sun	Memberships: _____
☐ Paved	☐ Sand / Grass	☐ Gravel	Ammenities:_____
☐ Picnic Table	☐ Fire ring	☐ Trees ☐ Lawn	

☐ Patio	☐ Kid Friendly	☐ Pet Friendly	Location	☺ 😐 ☹	Water Pressure	☺ 😐 ☹
☐ Store	☐ Cafe	☐ Firewood	Restrooms	☺ 😐 ☹	Laundry	☺ 😐 ☹
☐ Ice	☐ Security	☐ Quiet ☐ Noisy	Pool	☺ 😐 ☹	Hot Tub	☺ 😐 ☹

PLACES VISITED / ACTIVITIES: _____

_____

_____

PEOPLE MET / NEW FRIENDS: _____

_____

_____

FOOD, DINING & RESTAURANTS: _____

_____

_____

HIGHLIGHTS / MEMORABLE EVENTS: _____

_____

_____

PLACES TO GO & THINGS TO DO FOR NEXT TIME: _____

_____

_____

_____

NOTES:

Date: _____	From: _____	Beginning Mileage: _____
Weather:	To: _____	Ending Mileage: _____
☀ ⛅ ☔ ❄	Route Taken: _____	
🌡 🌡 📢 ☁	_____	Total Miles Traveled: _____

CAMPGROUND INFORMATION

Name: _____
Address: _____
Phone: _____

Site # _____ $ _____ ☐ Day ☐ Week ☐ Month

☐ First Visit ☐ Return Visit ☐ Easy Access
☐ Site Level ☐ Back-in ☐ Pull-through
☐ 15 amp ☐ 30 amp ☐ 50 amp
☐ Water ☐ Sewer ☐ Shade ☐ Sun
☐ Paved ☐ Sand / Grass ☐ Gravel
☐ Picnic Table ☐ Fire ring ☐ Trees ☐ Lawn
☐ Patio ☐ Kid Friendly ☐ Pet Friendly
☐ Store ☐ Cafe ☐ Firewood
☐ Ice ☐ Security ☐ Quiet ☐ Noisy

Our Rating: ☆ ☆ ☆ ☆ ☆
GPS: _____
Altitude: _____
Cell Service / Carrier: _____

☐ Antenna Reception ☐ Satellite TV ☐ Cable TV
☐ Wifi Available ☐ Free ☐ Fee $_____

Memberships: _____
Ammenities: _____

Location	☺	☺	☹	Water Pressure	☺	☺	☹
Restrooms	☺	☺	☹	Laundry	☺	☺	☹
Pool	☺	☺	☹	Hot Tub	☺	☺	☹

PLACES VISITED / ACTIVITIES: _____
_____
_____
_____

PEOPLE MET / NEW FRIENDS: _____
_____
_____
_____

FOOD, DINING & RESTAURANTS: _____
_____
_____
_____

HIGHLIGHTS / MEMORABLE EVENTS: _____
_____
_____
_____

PLACES TO GO & THINGS TO DO FOR NEXT TIME: _____
_____
_____
_____

NOTES:

Date: _____	From: _____	Beginning Mileage:
Weather:	To: _____	Ending Mileage:
☀ ⛅ ☂ ❄	Route Taken: _____	
🌡 🌡 🚩 ☁	_____	Total Miles Traveled:

CAMPGROUND INFORMATION

Name: _____

Our Rating: ☆ ☆ ☆ ☆ ☆

Address: _____

GPS: _____

Phone: _____

Altitude: _____

Site # _____ $ _____ ☐ Day ☐ Week ☐ Month

Cell Service / Carrier: _____

☐ First Visit ☐ Return Visit ☐ Easy Access
☐ Site Level ☐ Back-in ☐ Pull-through
☐ 15 amp ☐ 30 amp ☐ 50 amp
☐ Water ☐ Sewer ☐ Shade ☐ Sun
☐ Paved ☐ Sand / Grass ☐ Gravel
☐ Picnic Table ☐ Fire ring ☐ Trees ☐ Lawn
☐ Patio ☐ Kid Friendly ☐ Pet Friendly
☐ Store ☐ Cafe ☐ Firewood
☐ Ice ☐ Security ☐ Quiet ☐ Noisy

☐ Antenna Reception ☐ Satellite TV ☐ Cable TV
☐ Wifi Available ☐ Free ☐ Fee $ _____

Memberships: _____

Ammenities: _____

Location	☺	☺	☹	Water Pressure	☺	☺	☹
Restrooms	☺	☺	☹	Laundry	☺	☺	☹
Pool	☺	☺	☹	Hot Tub	☺	☺	☹

PLACES VISITED / ACTIVITIES: _____

_____

_____

_____

PEOPLE MET / NEW FRIENDS: _____

_____

_____

_____

FOOD, DINING & RESTAURANTS: _____

_____

_____

_____

HIGHLIGHTS / MEMORABLE EVENTS: _____

_____

_____

_____

PLACES TO GO & THINGS TO DO FOR NEXT TIME: _____

_____

_____

_____

NOTES:

Date: _____	From: _____	Beginning Mileage:
Weather:	To: _____	Ending Mileage:
☀ ⛅ ☔ ❄	Route Taken: _____	
🌡 🌡 🎐 🌩	_____	Total Miles Traveled:

CAMPGROUND INFORMATION

Name:_____

Address:_____

Phone:_____

Our Rating: ☆ ☆ ☆ ☆ ☆

GPS: _____

Altitude: _____

Site # _____ $ _____ ☐ Day ☐ Week ☐ Month

☐ First Visit	☐ Return Visit	☐ Easy Access
☐ Site Level	☐ Back-in	☐ Pull-through
☐ 15 amp	☐ 30 amp	☐ 50 amp
☐ Water	☐ Sewer	☐ Shade ☐ Sun
☐ Paved	☐ Sand / Grass	☐ Gravel
☐ Picnic Table	☐ Fire ring	☐ Trees ☐ Lawn
☐ Patio	☐ Kid Friendly	☐ Pet Friendly
☐ Store	☐ Cafe	☐ Firewood
☐ Ice	☐ Security	☐ Quiet ☐ Noisy

Cell Service / Carrier:_____

☐ Antenna Reception ☐ Satellite TV ☐ Cable TV

☐ Wifi Available ☐ Free ☐ Fee $_____

Memberships: _____

Amenities:_____

Location	☺ ☺ ☹	Water Pressure	☺ ☺ ☹
Restrooms	☺ ☺ ☹	Laundry	☺ ☺ ☹
Pool	☺ ☺ ☹	Hot Tub	☺ ☺ ☹

PLACES VISITED / ACTIVITIES:
_____
_____
_____
_____

PEOPLE MET / NEW FRIENDS:
_____
_____
_____
_____

FOOD, DINING & RESTAURANTS:
_____
_____
_____
_____

HIGHLIGHTS / MEMORABLE EVENTS:
_____
_____
_____
_____

PLACES TO GO & THINGS TO DO FOR NEXT TIME:
_____
_____
_____
_____

NOTES:

Date: _____	From: _____	Beginning Mileage:
	To: _____	_____
Weather:	Route Taken: _____	Ending Mileage:
☀ ⛅ ☔ ❄	_____	_____
🌡 ❄ 🎐 🌩		Total Miles Traveled:

CAMPGROUND INFORMATION

Name:_____	Our Rating: ☆ ☆ ☆ ☆ ☆
Address:_____	GPS: _____
Phone:_____	Altitude: _____
Site #_____ $_____ ☐ Day ☐ Week ☐ Month	Cell Service / Carrier:_____

☐ First Visit	☐ Return Visit	☐ Easy Access	☐ Antenna Reception ☐ Satellite TV ☐ Cable TV
☐ Site Level	☐ Back-in	☐ Pull-through	☐ Wifi Available ☐ Free ☐ Fee $_____
☐ 15 amp	☐ 30 amp	☐ 50 amp	
☐ Water	☐ Sewer	☐ Shade ☐ Sun	Memberships: _____
☐ Paved	☐ Sand / Grass	☐ Gravel	Ammenities:_____
☐ Picnic Table	☐ Fire ring	☐ Trees ☐ Lawn	Location ☺ ☺ ☹ Water Pressure ☺ ☺ ☹
☐ Patio	☐ Kid Friendly	☐ Pet Friendly	Restrooms ☺ ☺ ☹ Laundry ☺ ☺ ☹
☐ Store	☐ Cafe	☐ Firewood	Pool ☺ ☺ ☹ Hot Tub ☺ ☺ ☹
☐ Ice	☐ Security	☐ Quiet ☐ Noisy	

PLACES VISITED / ACTIVITIES: _____

_____

_____

_____

PEOPLE MET / NEW FRIENDS: _____

_____

_____

_____

FOOD, DINING & RESTAURANTS: _____

_____

_____

_____

HIGHLIGHTS / MEMORABLE EVENTS: _____

_____

_____

_____

PLACES TO GO & THINGS TO DO FOR NEXT TIME: _____

_____

_____

_____

NOTES:

Date: _____	From: _____	Beginning Mileage: _____
Weather:	To: _____	Ending Mileage: _____
☀ ⛅ ☂ ❄ 🌡 🌡 🎐 💭	Route Taken: _____ _____	Total Miles Traveled:

CAMPGROUND INFORMATION

Name:_____

Address:_____

Phone:_____

Our Rating: ☆ ☆ ☆ ☆ ☆

GPS: _____

Altitude: _____

Cell Service / Carrier:_____

Site #_____ $_____ ☐ Day ☐ Week ☐ Month

☐ First Visit	☐ Return Visit	☐ Easy Access
☐ Site Level	☐ Back-in	☐ Pull-through
☐ 15 amp	☐ 30 amp	☐ 50 amp
☐ Water	☐ Sewer	☐ Shade ☐ Sun
☐ Paved	☐ Sand / Grass	☐ Gravel
☐ Picnic Table	☐ Fire ring	☐ Trees ☐ Lawn
☐ Patio	☐ Kid Friendly	☐ Pet Friendly
☐ Store	☐ Cafe	☐ Firewood
☐ Ice	☐ Security	☐ Quiet ☐ Noisy

☐ Antenna Reception   ☐ Satellite TV   ☐ Cable TV
☐ Wifi Available   ☐ Free   ☐ Fee $_____

Memberships: _____

Ammenities:_____

Location	☺ ☻ ☹	Water Pressure	☺ ☻ ☹
Restrooms	☺ ☻ ☹	Laundry	☺ ☻ ☹
Pool	☺ ☻ ☹	Hot Tub	☺ ☻ ☹

PLACES VISITED / ACTIVITIES: _____

_____

_____

_____

PEOPLE MET / NEW FRIENDS: _____

_____

_____

_____

FOOD, DINING & RESTAURANTS: _____

_____

_____

_____

HIGHLIGHTS / MEMORABLE EVENTS: _____

_____

_____

_____

PLACES TO GO & THINGS TO DO FOR NEXT TIME: _____

_____

_____

_____

NOTES:

Date: _____	From: _____	Beginning Mileage:
Weather:	To: _____	Ending Mileage: _____
☀ ⛅ ☔ ❄	Route Taken: _____	
🌡 🌡 🎐 ☁	_____	Total Miles Traveled: _____

CAMPGROUND INFORMATION

Name: _____   Our Rating: ☆ ☆ ☆ ☆ ☆

Address: _____   GPS: _____

Phone: _____   Altitude: _____

Site # _____ $ _____   ☐ Day ☐ Week ☐ Month   Cell Service / Carrier: _____

☐ First Visit	☐ Return Visit	☐ Easy Access	☐ Antenna Reception ☐ Satellite TV ☐ Cable TV
☐ Site Level	☐ Back-in	☐ Pull-through	☐ Wifi Available ☐ Free ☐ Fee $ _____
☐ 15 amp	☐ 30 amp	☐ 50 amp	
☐ Water	☐ Sewer	☐ Shade ☐ Sun	Memberships: _____
☐ Paved	☐ Sand / Grass	☐ Gravel	Ammenities: _____
☐ Picnic Table	☐ Fire ring	☐ Trees ☐ Lawn	Location ☺ ☻ ☹ Water Pressure ☺ ☻ ☹
☐ Patio	☐ Kid Friendly	☐ Pet Friendly	Restrooms ☺ ☻ ☹ Laundry ☺ ☻ ☹
☐ Store	☐ Cafe	☐ Firewood	Pool ☺ ☻ ☹ Hot Tub ☺ ☻ ☹
☐ Ice	☐ Security	☐ Quiet ☐ Noisy	

PLACES VISITED / ACTIVITIES: _____

_____

_____

_____

PEOPLE MET / NEW FRIENDS: _____

_____

_____

_____

FOOD, DINING & RESTAURANTS: _____

_____

_____

_____

HIGHLIGHTS / MEMORABLE EVENTS: _____

_____

_____

_____

PLACES TO GO & THINGS TO DO FOR NEXT TIME: _____

_____

_____

_____

NOTES:

Date: _____	From: _____	Beginning Mileage:
	To: _____	_____
Weather:		Ending Mileage:
☀ ⛅ ☔ ❄	Route Taken: _____	_____
🌡 ❄ 🚩 💨	_____	Total Miles Traveled:

CAMPGROUND INFORMATION

Name:_____	Our Rating: ☆ ☆ ☆ ☆ ☆
Address:_____	GPS: _____
Phone:_____	Altitude: _____

Site #_____ $_____ ☐ Day ☐ Week ☐ Month

Cell Service / Carrier:_____

☐ First Visit	☐ Return Visit	☐ Easy Access
☐ Site Level	☐ Back-in	☐ Pull-through
☐ 15 amp	☐ 30 amp	☐ 50 amp
☐ Water	☐ Sewer	☐ Shade ☐ Sun
☐ Paved	☐ Sand / Grass	☐ Gravel
☐ Picnic Table	☐ Fire ring	☐ Trees ☐ Lawn
☐ Patio	☐ Kid Friendly	☐ Pet Friendly
☐ Store	☐ Cafe	☐ Firewood
☐ Ice	☐ Security	☐ Quiet ☐ Noisy

☐ Antenna Reception ☐ Satellite TV ☐ Cable TV
☐ Wifi Available ☐ Free ☐ Fee $_____

Memberships: _____

Ammenities:_____

Location	☺ ☺ ☹	Water Pressure	☺ ☺ ☹
Restrooms	☺ ☺ ☹	Laundry	☺ ☺ ☹
Pool	☺ ☺ ☹	Hot Tub	☺ ☺ ☹

PLACES VISITED / ACTIVITIES: _____
_____
_____
_____

PEOPLE MET / NEW FRIENDS: _____
_____
_____
_____

FOOD, DINING & RESTAURANTS: _____
_____
_____
_____

HIGHLIGHTS / MEMORABLE EVENTS: _____
_____
_____
_____

PLACES TO GO & THINGS TO DO FOR NEXT TIME: _____
_____
_____
_____

NOTES:

Date: _____	From: _____	Beginning Mileage: _____
Weather:	To: _____	Ending Mileage: _____
☀ ⛅ ☔ ❄	Route Taken: _____	
🌡 ❄🌡 🎐 ☁	_____	Total Miles Traveled:

CAMPGROUND INFORMATION

Name:_____	Our Rating: ☆ ☆ ☆ ☆ ☆
Address:_____	GPS: _____
Phone:_____	Altitude: _____
Site #_____ $_____ ☐ Day ☐ Week ☐ Month	Cell Service / Carrier:_____

☐ First Visit	☐ Return Visit	☐ Easy Access
☐ Site Level	☐ Back-in	☐ Pull-through
☐ 15 amp	☐ 30 amp	☐ 50 amp
☐ Water	☐ Sewer	☐ Shade ☐ Sun
☐ Paved	☐ Sand / Grass	☐ Gravel
☐ Picnic Table	☐ Fire ring	☐ Trees ☐ Lawn
☐ Patio	☐ Kid Friendly	☐ Pet Friendly
☐ Store	☐ Cafe	☐ Firewood
☐ Ice	☐ Security	☐ Quiet ☐ Noisy

☐ Antenna Reception ☐ Satellite TV ☐ Cable TV
☐ Wifi Available ☐ Free ☐ Fee $_____

Memberships: _____

Ammenities:_____

Location	☺ ☺ ☹	Water Pressure	☺ ☺ ☹
Restrooms	☺ ☺ ☹	Laundry	☺ ☺ ☹
Pool	☺ ☺ ☹	Hot Tub	☺ ☺ ☹

PLACES VISITED / ACTIVITIES: _____
_____
_____
_____

PEOPLE MET / NEW FRIENDS: _____
_____
_____
_____

FOOD, DINING & RESTAURANTS: _____
_____
_____
_____

HIGHLIGHTS / MEMORABLE EVENTS: _____
_____
_____
_____

PLACES TO GO & THINGS TO DO FOR NEXT TIME: _____
_____
_____
_____
_____

NOTES:

Date: _____	From: _____	Beginning Mileage: _____
Weather:	To: _____	Ending Mileage: _____
☀ ⛅ ☂ ❄ 🌡 🌡 📢 🌩	Route Taken: _____ _____	Total Miles Traveled: _____

CAMPGROUND INFORMATION

Name: _____

Address: _____

Phone: _____

Site # _____ $ _____ ☐ Day ☐ Week ☐ Month

☐ First Visit   ☐ Return Visit   ☐ Easy Access
☐ Site Level   ☐ Back-in   ☐ Pull-through
☐ 15 amp   ☐ 30 amp   ☐ 50 amp
☐ Water   ☐ Sewer   ☐ Shade ☐ Sun
☐ Paved   ☐ Sand / Grass   ☐ Gravel
☐ Picnic Table   ☐ Fire ring   ☐ Trees ☐ Lawn
☐ Patio   ☐ Kid Friendly   ☐ Pet Friendly
☐ Store   ☐ Cafe   ☐ Firewood
☐ Ice   ☐ Security   ☐ Quiet ☐ Noisy

Our Rating: ☆ ☆ ☆ ☆ ☆

GPS: _____

Altitude: _____

Cell Service / Carrier: _____

☐ Antenna Reception   ☐ Satellite TV   ☐ Cable TV
☐ Wifi Available   ☐ Free ☐ Fee $ _____

Memberships: _____

Ammenities: _____

Location	☺	☺	☹	Water Pressure	☺	☺	☹
Restrooms	☺	☺	☹	Laundry	☺	☺	☹
Pool	☺	☺	☹	Hot Tub	☺	☺	☹

PLACES VISITED / ACTIVITIES: _____

_____
_____
_____

PEOPLE MET / NEW FRIENDS: _____

_____
_____
_____

FOOD, DINING & RESTAURANTS: _____

_____
_____
_____

HIGHLIGHTS / MEMORABLE EVENTS: _____

_____
_____
_____

PLACES TO GO & THINGS TO DO FOR NEXT TIME: _____

_____
_____
_____

NOTES:

Date: _____

Weather:

☀ ⛅ ☔ ❄

🌡 ❄🌡 📢 🌩

From: _____

To: _____

Route Taken: _____

_____

Beginning Mileage:

_____

Ending Mileage:

_____

Total Miles Traveled:

CAMPGROUND INFORMATION

Name:_____

Address:_____

Phone:_____

Site #_____ $_____ ☐ Day ☐ Week ☐ Month

☐ First Visit   ☐ Return Visit   ☐ Easy Access
☐ Site Level   ☐ Back-in   ☐ Pull-through
☐ 15 amp   ☐ 30 amp   ☐ 50 amp
☐ Water   ☐ Sewer   ☐ Shade ☐ Sun
☐ Paved   ☐ Sand / Grass   ☐ Gravel
☐ Picnic Table   ☐ Fire ring   ☐ Trees ☐ Lawn
☐ Patio   ☐ Kid Friendly   ☐ Pet Friendly
☐ Store   ☐ Cafe   ☐ Firewood
☐ Ice   ☐ Security   ☐ Quiet ☐ Noisy

Our Rating: ☆ ☆ ☆ ☆ ☆

GPS: _____

Altitude: _____

Cell Service / Carrier:_____

☐ Antenna Reception   ☐ Satellite TV   ☐ Cable TV
☐ Wifi Available   ☐ Free ☐ Fee $_____

Memberships: _____

Ammenities:_____

Location	☺	😐	☹	Water Pressure	☺	😐	☹
Restrooms	☺	😐	☹	Laundry	☺	😐	☹
Pool	☺	😐	☹	Hot Tub	☺	😐	☹

PLACES VISITED / ACTIVITIES:

_____
_____
_____
_____

PEOPLE MET / NEW FRIENDS:

_____
_____
_____
_____

FOOD, DINING & RESTAURANTS:

_____
_____
_____
_____

HIGHLIGHTS / MEMORABLE EVENTS:

_____
_____
_____

PLACES TO GO & THINGS TO DO FOR NEXT TIME:

_____
_____
_____

NOTES:

Date: _____	From: _____	Beginning Mileage: _____
Weather:	To: _____	Ending Mileage: _____
☀ ⛅ ☔ ❄ 🌡 🌡 📯 ☁	Route Taken: _____ _____	Total Miles Traveled: _____

CAMPGROUND INFORMATION

Name: _____

Address: _____

Phone: _____

Site #_____ $_____ ☐ Day ☐ Week ☐ Month

☐ First Visit	☐ Return Visit	☐ Easy Access
☐ Site Level	☐ Back-in	☐ Pull-through
☐ 15 amp	☐ 30 amp	☐ 50 amp
☐ Water	☐ Sewer	☐ Shade ☐ Sun
☐ Paved	☐ Sand / Grass	☐ Gravel
☐ Picnic Table	☐ Fire ring	☐ Trees ☐ Lawn
☐ Patio	☐ Kid Friendly	☐ Pet Friendly
☐ Store	☐ Cafe	☐ Firewood
☐ Ice	☐ Security	☐ Quiet ☐ Noisy

Our Rating: ☆ ☆ ☆ ☆ ☆

GPS: _____

Altitude: _____

Cell Service / Carrier: _____

☐ Antenna Reception ☐ Satellite TV ☐ Cable TV
☐ Wifi Available ☐ Free ☐ Fee $_____

Memberships: _____

Ammenities: _____

Location	☺	☺	☹	Water Pressure	☺	☺	☹
Restrooms	☺	☺	☹	Laundry	☺	☺	☹
Pool	☺	☺	☹	Hot Tub	☺	☺	☹

PLACES VISITED / ACTIVITIES:
_____
_____
_____
_____

PEOPLE MET / NEW FRIENDS:
_____
_____
_____
_____

FOOD, DINING & RESTAURANTS:
_____
_____
_____
_____

HIGHLIGHTS / MEMORABLE EVENTS:
_____
_____
_____
_____

PLACES TO GO & THINGS TO DO FOR NEXT TIME:
_____
_____
_____
_____

NOTES:

Date: _____	From: _____	Beginning Mileage: _____
Weather: ☀ ⛅ ☂ ❄ 🌡 🌡 🚩 💨	To: _____ Route Taken: _____ _____	Ending Mileage: _____ Total Miles Traveled:

CAMPGROUND INFORMATION

Name: _____

Address: _____

Phone: _____

Site #_____ $_____ ☐ Day ☐ Week ☐ Month

☐ First Visit ☐ Return Visit ☐ Easy Access
☐ Site Level ☐ Back-in ☐ Pull-through
☐ 15 amp ☐ 30 amp ☐ 50 amp
☐ Water ☐ Sewer ☐ Shade ☐ Sun
☐ Paved ☐ Sand / Grass ☐ Gravel
☐ Picnic Table ☐ Fire ring ☐ Trees ☐ Lawn
☐ Patio ☐ Kid Friendly ☐ Pet Friendly
☐ Store ☐ Cafe ☐ Firewood
☐ Ice ☐ Security ☐ Quiet ☐ Noisy

Our Rating: ☆ ☆ ☆ ☆ ☆

GPS: _____

Altitude: _____

Cell Service / Carrier: _____

☐ Antenna Reception ☐ Satellite TV ☐ Cable TV
☐ Wifi Available ☐ Free ☐ Fee $_____

Memberships: _____

Ammenities: _____

Location	🙂	😐	🙁	Water Pressure	🙂	😐	🙁
Restrooms	🙂	😐	🙁	Laundry	🙂	😐	🙁
Pool	🙂	😐	🙁	Hot Tub	🙂	😐	🙁

PLACES VISITED / ACTIVITIES: _____

_____

_____

_____

PEOPLE MET / NEW FRIENDS: _____

_____

_____

_____

FOOD, DINING & RESTAURANTS: _____

_____

_____

_____

HIGHLIGHTS / MEMORABLE EVENTS: _____

_____

_____

_____

PLACES TO GO & THINGS TO DO FOR NEXT TIME: _____

_____

_____

_____

NOTES:

Date: _____	From: _____	Beginning Mileage:
Weather:	To: _____	_____
☀ ⛅ ☔ ❄	Route Taken: _____	Ending Mileage:
🌡 🌡 🚩 💨	_____	_____
		Total Miles Traveled:

CAMPGROUND INFORMATION

Name: _____	Our Rating: ☆ ☆ ☆ ☆ ☆
Address: _____	GPS: _____
Phone: _____	Altitude: _____

Site # _____ $ _____ ☐ Day ☐ Week ☐ Month

Cell Service / Carrier: _____

☐ First Visit ☐ Return Visit ☐ Easy Access
☐ Site Level ☐ Back-in ☐ Pull-through
☐ 15 amp ☐ 30 amp ☐ 50 amp
☐ Water ☐ Sewer ☐ Shade ☐ Sun
☐ Paved ☐ Sand / Grass ☐ Gravel
☐ Picnic Table ☐ Fire ring ☐ Trees ☐ Lawn
☐ Patio ☐ Kid Friendly ☐ Pet Friendly
☐ Store ☐ Cafe ☐ Firewood
☐ Ice ☐ Security ☐ Quiet ☐ Noisy

☐ Antenna Reception ☐ Satellite TV ☐ Cable TV
☐ Wifi Available ☐ Free ☐ Fee $_____

Memberships: _____

Ammenities: _____

Location	☺	☺	☹	Water Pressure	☺	☺	☹
Restrooms	☺	☺	☹	Laundry	☺	☺	☹
Pool	☺	☺	☹	Hot Tub	☺	☺	☹

PLACES VISITED / ACTIVITIES: _____
_____
_____
_____

PEOPLE MET / NEW FRIENDS: _____
_____
_____
_____

FOOD, DINING & RESTAURANTS: _____
_____
_____
_____

HIGHLIGHTS / MEMORABLE EVENTS: _____
_____
_____
_____

PLACES TO GO & THINGS TO DO FOR NEXT TIME: _____
_____
_____
_____

NOTES:

Date: _____	From: _____	Beginning Mileage: _____
Weather:	To: _____	Ending Mileage: _____
☀ ⛅ ☔ ❄	Route Taken: _____	
🌡 🌡 🚩 💭	_____	Total Miles Traveled: _____

CAMPGROUND INFORMATION

Name: _____

Our Rating: ☆ ☆ ☆ ☆ ☆

Address: _____

GPS: _____

Phone: _____

Altitude: _____

Site # _____ $ _____ ☐ Day ☐ Week ☐ Month

Cell Service / Carrier: _____

☐ First Visit ☐ Return Visit ☐ Easy Access
☐ Site Level ☐ Back-in ☐ Pull-through
☐ 15 amp ☐ 30 amp ☐ 50 amp
☐ Water ☐ Sewer ☐ Shade ☐ Sun
☐ Paved ☐ Sand / Grass ☐ Gravel
☐ Picnic Table ☐ Fire ring ☐ Trees ☐ Lawn
☐ Patio ☐ Kid Friendly ☐ Pet Friendly
☐ Store ☐ Cafe ☐ Firewood
☐ Ice ☐ Security ☐ Quiet ☐ Noisy

☐ Antenna Reception ☐ Satellite TV ☐ Cable TV
☐ Wifi Available ☐ Free ☐ Fee $ _____

Memberships: _____

Ammenities: _____

Location	☺	☺	☹	Water Pressure	☺ ☺ ☹
Restrooms	☺	☺	☹	Laundry	☺ ☺ ☹
Pool	☺	☺	☹	Hot Tub	☺ ☺ ☹

PLACES VISITED / ACTIVITIES: _____
_____
_____
_____

PEOPLE MET / NEW FRIENDS: _____
_____
_____
_____

FOOD, DINING & RESTAURANTS: _____
_____
_____
_____

HIGHLIGHTS / MEMORABLE EVENTS: _____
_____
_____
_____

PLACES TO GO & THINGS TO DO FOR NEXT TIME: _____
_____
_____
_____

NOTES:

Date: _____	From: _____	Beginning Mileage: _____
Weather:	To: _____	Ending Mileage: _____
	Route Taken: _____	
	_____	Total Miles Traveled: _____

CAMPGROUND INFORMATION

Name: _____

Address: _____

Phone: _____

Site # _____ $ _____ ☐ Day ☐ Week ☐ Month

☐ First Visit ☐ Return Visit ☐ Easy Access
☐ Site Level ☐ Back-in ☐ Pull-through
☐ 15 amp ☐ 30 amp ☐ 50 amp
☐ Water ☐ Sewer ☐ Shade ☐ Sun
☐ Paved ☐ Sand / Grass ☐ Gravel
☐ Picnic Table ☐ Fire ring ☐ Trees ☐ Lawn
☐ Patio ☐ Kid Friendly ☐ Pet Friendly
☐ Store ☐ Cafe ☐ Firewood
☐ Ice ☐ Security ☐ Quiet ☐ Noisy

Our Rating: ☆ ☆ ☆ ☆ ☆

GPS: _____

Altitude: _____

Cell Service / Carrier: _____

☐ Antenna Reception ☐ Satellite TV ☐ Cable TV
☐ Wifi Available ☐ Free ☐ Fee $ _____

Memberships: _____

Ammenities: _____

Location	☺	😐	☹	Water Pressure	☺	😐	☹
Restrooms	☺	😐	☹	Laundry	☺	😐	☹
Pool	☺	😐	☹	Hot Tub	☺	😐	☹

PLACES VISITED / ACTIVITIES: _____

_____

_____

_____

PEOPLE MET / NEW FRIENDS: _____

_____

_____

_____

FOOD, DINING & RESTAURANTS: _____

_____

_____

_____

HIGHLIGHTS / MEMORABLE EVENTS: _____

_____

_____

_____

PLACES TO GO & THINGS TO DO FOR NEXT TIME: _____

_____

_____

_____

NOTES:

Date: _____   From: _____   Beginning Mileage: _____

Weather: To: _____   Ending Mileage: _____
☀ ⛅ ☂ ❄   Route Taken: _____
🌡 ❄ 📢 ☁   _____   Total Miles Traveled: _____

CAMPGROUND INFORMATION

Name: _____   Our Rating: ☆ ☆ ☆ ☆ ☆

Address: _____   GPS: _____

Phone: _____   Altitude: _____

Site # _____ $ _____ ☐ Day ☐ Week ☐ Month   Cell Service / Carrier: _____

☐ First Visit	☐ Return Visit	☐ Easy Access
☐ Site Level	☐ Back-in	☐ Pull-through
☐ 15 amp	☐ 30 amp	☐ 50 amp
☐ Water	☐ Sewer	☐ Shade ☐ Sun
☐ Paved	☐ Sand / Grass	☐ Gravel
☐ Picnic Table	☐ Fire ring	☐ Trees ☐ Lawn
☐ Patio	☐ Kid Friendly	☐ Pet Friendly
☐ Store	☐ Cafe	☐ Firewood
☐ Ice	☐ Security	☐ Quiet ☐ Noisy

☐ Antenna Reception   ☐ Satellite TV   ☐ Cable TV
☐ Wifi Available   ☐ Free ☐ Fee $_____

Memberships: _____

Ammenities: _____

Location	☺	😐	☹	Water Pressure	☺	😐	☹
Restrooms	☺	😐	☹	Laundry	☺	😐	☹
Pool	☺	😐	☹	Hot Tub	☺	😐	☹

PLACES VISITED / ACTIVITIES:
_____
_____
_____
_____

PEOPLE MET / NEW FRIENDS:
_____
_____
_____
_____

FOOD, DINING & RESTAURANTS:
_____
_____
_____
_____

HIGHLIGHTS / MEMORABLE EVENTS:
_____
_____
_____
_____

PLACES TO GO & THINGS TO DO FOR NEXT TIME:
_____
_____
_____
_____

NOTES:

Date: _____

Weather:

From: _____

To: _____

Route Taken: _____

_____

Beginning Mileage: _____

Ending Mileage: _____

Total Miles Traveled:

CAMPGROUND INFORMATION

Name: _____

Address: _____

Phone: _____

Site # _____ $ _____ ☐ Day ☐ Week ☐ Month

☐ First Visit   ☐ Return Visit   ☐ Easy Access
☐ Site Level   ☐ Back-in   ☐ Pull-through
☐ 15 amp   ☐ 30 amp   ☐ 50 amp
☐ Water   ☐ Sewer   ☐ Shade   ☐ Sun
☐ Paved   ☐ Sand / Grass   ☐ Gravel
☐ Picnic Table ☐ Fire ring   ☐ Trees   ☐ Lawn
☐ Patio   ☐ Kid Friendly   ☐ Pet Friendly
☐ Store   ☐ Cafe   ☐ Firewood
☐ Ice   ☐ Security   ☐ Quiet   ☐ Noisy

Our Rating: ☆ ☆ ☆ ☆ ☆

GPS: _____

Altitude: _____

Cell Service / Carrier: _____

☐ Antenna Reception   ☐ Satellite TV   ☐ Cable TV
☐ Wifi Available   ☐ Free ☐ Fee $_____

Memberships: _____

Ammenities: _____

Location   ☺ ☻ ☹   Water Pressure ☺ ☻ ☹
Restrooms   ☺ ☻ ☹   Laundry   ☺ ☻ ☹
Pool   ☺ ☻ ☹   Hot Tub   ☺ ☻ ☹

PLACES VISITED / ACTIVITIES:

_____
_____
_____
_____

PEOPLE MET / NEW FRIENDS:

_____
_____
_____
_____

FOOD, DINING & RESTAURANTS:

_____
_____
_____
_____

HIGHLIGHTS / MEMORABLE EVENTS:

_____
_____
_____
_____

PLACES TO GO & THINGS TO DO FOR NEXT TIME:

_____
_____
_____
_____

NOTES:

Date: _____	From: _____	Beginning Mileage: _____
Weather:	To: _____	Ending Mileage: _____
☀ ⛅ ☔ ❄ / 🌡 ❄ 🚩 ☁	Route Taken: _____	Total Miles Traveled: _____

Campground Information

Name:_____	Our Rating: ☆ ☆ ☆ ☆ ☆
Address:_____	GPS: _____
Phone:_____	Altitude: _____
Site #_____ $_____ ☐ Day ☐ Week ☐ Month	Cell Service / Carrier:_____

☐ First Visit	☐ Return Visit	☐ Easy Access	☐ Antenna Reception ☐ Satellite TV ☐ Cable TV
☐ Site Level	☐ Back-in	☐ Pull-through	☐ Wifi Available ☐ Free ☐ Fee $_____
☐ 15 amp	☐ 30 amp	☐ 50 amp	Memberships: _____
☐ Water	☐ Sewer	☐ Shade ☐ Sun	Ammenities:_____
☐ Paved	☐ Sand / Grass	☐ Gravel	
☐ Picnic Table	☐ Fire ring	☐ Trees ☐ Lawn	Location ☺ ☹ ☹ Water Pressure ☺ ☹ ☹
☐ Patio	☐ Kid Friendly	☐ Pet Friendly	Restrooms ☺ ☹ ☹ Laundry ☺ ☹ ☹
☐ Store	☐ Cafe	☐ Firewood	Pool ☺ ☹ ☹ Hot Tub ☺ ☹ ☹
☐ Ice	☐ Security	☐ Quiet ☐ Noisy	

Places Visited / Activities:
_____
_____
_____
_____

People Met / New Friends:
_____
_____
_____
_____

Food, Dining & Restaurants:
_____
_____
_____
_____

Highlights / Memorable Events:
_____
_____
_____
_____

Places To Go & Things To Do for Next Time:
_____
_____
_____
_____

NOTES:

Date: _____	From: _____	Beginning Mileage:
	To: _____	_____
Weather:	Route Taken: _____	Ending Mileage:
☀ ⛅ ☔ ❄	_____	_____
🌡 🌡 🎐 ☁		Total Miles Traveled:

CAMPGROUND INFORMATION

Name:_____	Our Rating: ☆ ☆ ☆ ☆ ☆
Address:_____	GPS: _____
Phone:_____	Altitude: _____
Site #_____ $_____ ☐ Day ☐ Week ☐ Month	Cell Service / Carrier:_____

☐ First Visit	☐ Return Visit	☐ Easy Access
☐ Site Level	☐ Back-in	☐ Pull-through
☐ 15 amp	☐ 30 amp	☐ 50 amp
☐ Water	☐ Sewer	☐ Shade ☐ Sun
☐ Paved	☐ Sand / Grass	☐ Gravel
☐ Picnic Table	☐ Fire ring	☐ Trees ☐ Lawn
☐ Patio	☐ Kid Friendly	☐ Pet Friendly
☐ Store	☐ Cafe	☐ Firewood
☐ Ice	☐ Security	☐ Quiet ☐ Noisy

☐ Antenna Reception ☐ Satellite TV ☐ Cable TV
☐ Wifi Available ☐ Free ☐ Fee $_____

Memberships: _____

Ammenities:_____

Location	☺ 😐 ☹	Water Pressure	☺ 😐 ☹
Restrooms	☺ 😐 ☹	Laundry	☺ 😐 ☹
Pool	☺ 😐 ☹	Hot Tub	☺ 😐 ☹

PLACES VISITED / ACTIVITIES: _____

_____

_____

_____

PEOPLE MET / NEW FRIENDS: _____

_____

_____

_____

FOOD, DINING & RESTAURANTS: _____

_____

_____

_____

HIGHLIGHTS / MEMORABLE EVENTS: _____

_____

_____

_____

PLACES TO GO & THINGS TO DO FOR NEXT TIME: _____

_____

_____

_____

NOTES:

Date: _____	From: _____	Beginning Mileage: _____
Weather: ☀ ☁ ☂ ❄ 🌡 🌡 🚩 💭	To: _____ Route Taken: _____ _____	Ending Mileage: _____ Total Miles Traveled: _____

Campground Information

Name:_____	Our Rating: ☆ ☆ ☆ ☆ ☆
Address:_____	GPS: _____
Phone:_____	Altitude: _____

Site # _____ $_____ ☐ Day ☐ Week ☐ Month

Cell Service / Carrier:_____

☐ First Visit	☐ Return Visit	☐ Easy Access	
☐ Site Level	☐ Back-in	☐ Pull-through	
☐ 15 amp	☐ 30 amp	☐ 50 amp	
☐ Water	☐ Sewer	☐ Shade ☐ Sun	
☐ Paved	☐ Sand / Grass	☐ Gravel	
☐ Picnic Table	☐ Fire ring	☐ Trees ☐ Lawn	
☐ Patio	☐ Kid Friendly	☐ Pet Friendly	
☐ Store	☐ Cafe	☐ Firewood	
☐ Ice	☐ Security	☐ Quiet ☐ Noisy	

☐ Antenna Reception ☐ Satellite TV ☐ Cable TV
☐ Wifi Available ☐ Free ☐ Fee $_____

Memberships: _____
Ammenities:_____

Location	☺ ☺ ☹	Water Pressure	☺ ☺ ☹
Restrooms	☺ ☺ ☹	Laundry	☺ ☺ ☹
Pool	☺ ☺ ☹	Hot Tub	☺ ☺ ☹

Places Visited / Activities:
_____
_____
_____
_____

People Met / New Friends:
_____
_____
_____
_____

Food, Dining & Restaurants:
_____
_____
_____
_____

Highlights / Memorable Events:
_____
_____
_____
_____

Places To Go & Things To Do for Next Time:
_____
_____
_____
_____

NOTES:

Date: _____	From: _____	Beginning Mileage: _____
Weather:	To: _____	Ending Mileage: _____
☀ ⛅ ☔ ❄ / 🌡 🌡 🎐 ☁	Route Taken: _____ _____	Total Miles Traveled:

CAMPGROUND INFORMATION

Name: _____   Our Rating: ☆ ☆ ☆ ☆ ☆

Address: _____   GPS: _____

Phone: _____   Altitude: _____

Site # _____ $ _____ ☐ Day ☐ Week ☐ Month | Cell Service / Carrier: _____

☐ First Visit   ☐ Return Visit   ☐ Easy Access   ☐ Antenna Reception   ☐ Satellite TV   ☐ Cable TV
☐ Site Level   ☐ Back-in   ☐ Pull-through   ☐ Wifi Available   ☐ Free ☐ Fee $ _____
☐ 15 amp   ☐ 30 amp   ☐ 50 amp
☐ Water   ☐ Sewer   ☐ Shade ☐ Sun   Memberships: _____
☐ Paved   ☐ Sand / Grass   ☐ Gravel   Ammenities: _____
☐ Picnic Table   ☐ Fire ring   ☐ Trees ☐ Lawn
☐ Patio   ☐ Kid Friendly   ☐ Pet Friendly   Location   ☺ ☹ 😣   Water Pressure ☺ ☹ 😣
☐ Store   ☐ Cafe   ☐ Firewood   Restrooms ☺ ☹ 😣   Laundry   ☺ ☹ 😣
☐ Ice   ☐ Security   ☐ Quiet ☐ Noisy   Pool   ☺ ☹ 😣   Hot Tub   ☺ ☹ 😣

PLACES VISITED / ACTIVITIES:
_____
_____
_____
_____

PEOPLE MET / NEW FRIENDS:
_____
_____
_____
_____

FOOD, DINING & RESTAURANTS:
_____
_____
_____
_____

HIGHLIGHTS / MEMORABLE EVENTS:
_____
_____
_____
_____

PLACES TO GO & THINGS TO DO FOR NEXT TIME:
_____
_____
_____
_____

NOTES:

Date: _____ From: _____ Beginning Mileage: _____

Weather: _____ To: _____ Ending Mileage: _____

☀ ⛅ ☔ ❄ Route Taken: _____

🌡 ❄🌡 🚩 💭 _____ Total Miles Traveled: _____

CAMPGROUND INFORMATION

Name: _____

Address: _____

Phone: _____

Site # _____ $ _____ ☐ Day ☐ Week ☐ Month

☐ First Visit   ☐ Return Visit   ☐ Easy Access
☐ Site Level   ☐ Back-in   ☐ Pull-through
☐ 15 amp   ☐ 30 amp   ☐ 50 amp
☐ Water   ☐ Sewer   ☐ Shade   ☐ Sun
☐ Paved   ☐ Sand / Grass   ☐ Gravel
☐ Picnic Table   ☐ Fire ring   ☐ Trees   ☐ Lawn
☐ Patio   ☐ Kid Friendly   ☐ Pet Friendly
☐ Store   ☐ Cafe   ☐ Firewood
☐ Ice   ☐ Security   ☐ Quiet   ☐ Noisy

Our Rating: ☆ ☆ ☆ ☆ ☆

GPS: _____

Altitude: _____

Cell Service / Carrier: _____

☐ Antenna Reception   ☐ Satellite TV   ☐ Cable TV
☐ Wifi Available   ☐ Free ☐ Fee $_____

Memberships: _____

Ammenities: _____

Location	☺	😐	☹	Water Pressure	☺	😐	☹
Restrooms	☺	😐	☹	Laundry	☺	😐	☹
Pool	☺	😐	☹	Hot Tub	☺	😐	☹

PLACES VISITED / ACTIVITIES: _____
_____
_____
_____

PEOPLE MET / NEW FRIENDS: _____
_____
_____
_____

FOOD, DINING & RESTAURANTS: _____
_____
_____
_____

HIGHLIGHTS / MEMORABLE EVENTS: _____
_____
_____
_____

PLACES TO GO & THINGS TO DO FOR NEXT TIME: _____
_____
_____
_____

NOTES:

Date: _____	From: _____	Beginning Mileage:
Weather:	To: _____	Ending Mileage:
☀ ☁ ☂ ❄	Route Taken: _____	
🌡 🌡 🚩 ☁	_____	Total Miles Traveled:

CAMPGROUND INFORMATION

Name:_____

Address:_____

Phone:_____

Site #_____ $_____ ☐ Day ☐ Week ☐ Month

☐ First Visit	☐ Return Visit	☐ Easy Access
☐ Site Level	☐ Back-in	☐ Pull-through
☐ 15 amp	☐ 30 amp	☐ 50 amp
☐ Water	☐ Sewer	☐ Shade ☐ Sun
☐ Paved	☐ Sand / Grass	☐ Gravel
☐ Picnic Table	☐ Fire ring	☐ Trees ☐ Lawn
☐ Patio	☐ Kid Friendly	☐ Pet Friendly
☐ Store	☐ Cafe	☐ Firewood
☐ Ice	☐ Security	☐ Quiet ☐ Noisy

Our Rating: ☆ ☆ ☆ ☆ ☆

GPS: _____

Altitude: _____

Cell Service / Carrier: _____

☐ Antenna Reception ☐ Satellite TV ☐ Cable TV
☐ Wifi Available ☐ Free ☐ Fee $_____

Memberships: _____

Ammenities:_____

Location	☺ ☺ ☹	Water Pressure	☺ ☺ ☹
Restrooms	☺ ☺ ☹	Laundry	☺ ☺ ☹
Pool	☺ ☺ ☹	Hot Tub	☺ ☺ ☹

PLACES VISITED / ACTIVITIES: _____

_____
_____
_____
_____

PEOPLE MET / NEW FRIENDS: _____

_____
_____
_____
_____

FOOD, DINING & RESTAURANTS: _____

_____
_____
_____
_____

HIGHLIGHTS / MEMORABLE EVENTS: _____

_____
_____
_____
_____

PLACES TO GO & THINGS TO DO FOR NEXT TIME: _____

_____
_____
_____
_____

NOTES:

Date: _____	From: _____	Beginning Mileage: _____
Weather:	To: _____	Ending Mileage: _____
	Route Taken: _____	Total Miles Traveled: _____

CAMPGROUND INFORMATION

Name: _____

Address: _____

Phone: _____

Site # _____ $ _____ ☐ Day ☐ Week ☐ Month

☐ First Visit	☐ Return Visit	☐ Easy Access
☐ Site Level	☐ Back-in	☐ Pull-through
☐ 15 amp	☐ 30 amp	☐ 50 amp
☐ Water	☐ Sewer	☐ Shade ☐ Sun
☐ Paved	☐ Sand / Grass	☐ Gravel
☐ Picnic Table	☐ Fire ring	☐ Trees ☐ Lawn
☐ Patio	☐ Kid Friendly	☐ Pet Friendly
☐ Store	☐ Cafe	☐ Firewood
☐ Ice	☐ Security	☐ Quiet ☐ Noisy

Our Rating: ☆ ☆ ☆ ☆ ☆

GPS: _____

Altitude: _____

Cell Service / Carrier: _____

☐ Antenna Reception ☐ Satellite TV ☐ Cable TV
☐ Wifi Available ☐ Free ☐ Fee $ _____

Memberships: _____

Ammenities: _____

Location	☺ ☺ ☹	Water Pressure	☺ ☺ ☹
Restrooms	☺ ☺ ☹	Laundry	☺ ☺ ☹
Pool	☺ ☺ ☹	Hot Tub	☺ ☺ ☹

PLACES VISITED / ACTIVITIES:
_____
_____
_____
_____

PEOPLE MET / NEW FRIENDS:
_____
_____
_____
_____

FOOD, DINING & RESTAURANTS:
_____
_____
_____
_____

HIGHLIGHTS / MEMORABLE EVENTS:
_____
_____
_____
_____

PLACES TO GO & THINGS TO DO FOR NEXT TIME:
_____
_____
_____
_____

NOTES:

Date: _____	From: _____	Beginning Mileage: _____
Weather:	To: _____	Ending Mileage: _____
☀ ⛅ ☔ ❄	Route Taken: _____	Total Miles Traveled: _____
🌡 ❄🌡 🚩 ☁	_____	

CAMPGROUND INFORMATION

Name: _____

Address: _____

Phone: _____

Site #_____ $_____ ☐ Day ☐ Week ☐ Month

☐ First Visit ☐ Return Visit ☐ Easy Access
☐ Site Level ☐ Back-in ☐ Pull-through
☐ 15 amp ☐ 30 amp ☐ 50 amp
☐ Water ☐ Sewer ☐ Shade ☐ Sun
☐ Paved ☐ Sand / Grass ☐ Gravel
☐ Picnic Table ☐ Fire ring ☐ Trees ☐ Lawn
☐ Patio ☐ Kid Friendly ☐ Pet Friendly
☐ Store ☐ Cafe ☐ Firewood
☐ Ice ☐ Security ☐ Quiet ☐ Noisy

Our Rating: ☆ ☆ ☆ ☆ ☆

GPS: _____

Altitude: _____

Cell Service / Carrier: _____

☐ Antenna Reception ☐ Satellite TV ☐ Cable TV
☐ Wifi Available ☐ Free ☐ Fee $_____

Memberships: _____

Ammenities: _____

Location	☺	😐	☹	Water Pressure	☺	😐	☹
Restrooms	☺	😐	☹	Laundry	☺	😐	☹
Pool	☺	😐	☹	Hot Tub	☺	😐	☹

PLACES VISITED / ACTIVITIES: _____
_____
_____
_____
_____

PEOPLE MET / NEW FRIENDS: _____
_____
_____
_____
_____

FOOD, DINING & RESTAURANTS: _____
_____
_____
_____
_____

HIGHLIGHTS / MEMORABLE EVENTS: _____
_____
_____
_____
_____

PLACES TO GO & THINGS TO DO FOR NEXT TIME: _____
_____
_____
_____
_____

NOTES:

Date: _____	From: _____	Beginning Mileage:
Weather:	To: _____	_____
☀ ☁ ☂ ❄	Route Taken: _____	Ending Mileage:
🌡 🌡 🚩 ☁	_____	Total Miles Traveled:

Campground Information

Name: _____	Our Rating: ☆ ☆ ☆ ☆ ☆
Address: _____	GPS: _____
Phone: _____	Altitude: _____

Site # _____ $ _____ ☐ Day ☐ Week ☐ Month | Cell Service / Carrier: _____

☐ First Visit   ☐ Return Visit   ☐ Easy Access
☐ Site Level   ☐ Back-in   ☐ Pull-through
☐ 15 amp   ☐ 30 amp   ☐ 50 amp
☐ Water   ☐ Sewer   ☐ Shade ☐ Sun
☐ Paved   ☐ Sand / Grass   ☐ Gravel
☐ Picnic Table ☐ Fire ring   ☐ Trees ☐ Lawn
☐ Patio   ☐ Kid Friendly   ☐ Pet Friendly
☐ Store   ☐ Cafe   ☐ Firewood
☐ Ice   ☐ Security   ☐ Quiet ☐ Noisy

☐ Antenna Reception   ☐ Satellite TV   ☐ Cable TV
☐ Wifi Available   ☐ Free ☐ Fee $_____

Memberships: _____
Ammenities: _____

Location	☺	☺	☹	Water Pressure	☺	☺	☹
Restrooms	☺	☺	☹	Laundry	☺	☺	☹
Pool	☺	☺	☹	Hot Tub	☺	☺	☹

Places Visited / Activities: _____

_____
_____
_____

People Met / New Friends: _____

_____
_____
_____

Food, Dining & Restaurants: _____

_____
_____
_____

Highlights / Memorable Events: _____

_____
_____
_____

Places To Go & Things To Do for Next Time: _____

_____
_____
_____
_____

NOTES:

Date: _____

Weather:

☀ ⛅ ☔ ❄
🌡 🌡 🚩 🌩

From: _____

To: _____

Route Taken: _____

_____

Beginning Mileage: _____

Ending Mileage: _____

Total Miles Traveled:

CAMPGROUND INFORMATION

Name: _____

Address: _____

Phone: _____

Our Rating: ☆ ☆ ☆ ☆ ☆

GPS: _____

Altitude: _____

Site # _____ $ _____ ☐ Day ☐ Week ☐ Month

Cell Service / Carrier: _____

☐ First Visit	☐ Return Visit	☐ Easy Access
☐ Site Level	☐ Back-in	☐ Pull-through
☐ 15 amp	☐ 30 amp	☐ 50 amp
☐ Water	☐ Sewer	☐ Shade ☐ Sun
☐ Paved	☐ Sand / Grass	☐ Gravel
☐ Picnic Table	☐ Fire ring	☐ Trees ☐ Lawn
☐ Patio	☐ Kid Friendly	☐ Pet Friendly
☐ Store	☐ Cafe	☐ Firewood
☐ Ice	☐ Security	☐ Quiet ☐ Noisy

☐ Antenna Reception ☐ Satellite TV ☐ Cable TV
☐ Wifi Available ☐ Free ☐ Fee $_____

Memberships: _____

Ammenities: _____

Location	☺	😐	☹	Water Pressure	☺	😐	☹
Restrooms	☺	😐	☹	Laundry	☺	😐	☹
Pool	☺	😐	☹	Hot Tub	☺	😐	☹

PLACES VISITED / ACTIVITIES: _____

_____

_____

_____

PEOPLE MET / NEW FRIENDS: _____

_____

_____

_____

FOOD, DINING & RESTAURANTS: _____

_____

_____

_____

HIGHLIGHTS / MEMORABLE EVENTS: _____

_____

_____

_____

PLACES TO GO & THINGS TO DO FOR NEXT TIME: _____

_____

_____

_____

NOTES:

Date: _____	From: _____	Beginning Mileage: _____
Weather:	To: _____	Ending Mileage: _____
☀ ⛅ ☂ ❄ 🌡 🌡 📣 💭	Route Taken: _____ _____	Total Miles Traveled: _____

CAMPGROUND INFORMATION

Name: _____

Address: _____

Phone: _____

Site # _____ $ _____ ☐ Day ☐ Week ☐ Month

☐ First Visit	☐ Return Visit	☐ Easy Access
☐ Site Level	☐ Back-in	☐ Pull-through
☐ 15 amp	☐ 30 amp	☐ 50 amp
☐ Water	☐ Sewer	☐ Shade ☐ Sun
☐ Paved	☐ Sand / Grass	☐ Gravel
☐ Picnic Table	☐ Fire ring	☐ Trees ☐ Lawn
☐ Patio	☐ Kid Friendly	☐ Pet Friendly
☐ Store	☐ Cafe	☐ Firewood
☐ Ice	☐ Security	☐ Quiet ☐ Noisy

Our Rating: ☆ ☆ ☆ ☆ ☆

GPS: _____

Altitude: _____

Cell Service / Carrier: _____

☐ Antenna Reception   ☐ Satellite TV   ☐ Cable TV
☐ Wifi Available   ☐ Free ☐ Fee $_____

Memberships: _____

Ammenities: _____

Location	☺	☺	☹	Water Pressure	☺	☺	☹
Restrooms	☺	☺	☹	Laundry	☺	☺	☹
Pool	☺	☺	☹	Hot Tub	☺	☺	☹

PLACES VISITED / ACTIVITIES:
_____
_____
_____
_____

PEOPLE MET / NEW FRIENDS:
_____
_____
_____
_____

FOOD, DINING & RESTAURANTS:
_____
_____
_____
_____

HIGHLIGHTS / MEMORABLE EVENTS:
_____
_____
_____

PLACES TO GO & THINGS TO DO FOR NEXT TIME:
_____
_____
_____

NOTES:

Date: _____

Weather:

☀ ⛅ ☔ ❄
🌡 🌡 🎐 ☁

From: _____

To: _____

Route Taken: _____

_____

Beginning Mileage: _____

Ending Mileage: _____

Total Miles Traveled: _____

CAMPGROUND INFORMATION

Name: _____

Address: _____

Phone: _____

Site #_____ $_____ ☐ Day ☐ Week ☐ Month

☐ First Visit   ☐ Return Visit   ☐ Easy Access
☐ Site Level   ☐ Back-in   ☐ Pull-through
☐ 15 amp   ☐ 30 amp   ☐ 50 amp
☐ Water   ☐ Sewer   ☐ Shade   ☐ Sun
☐ Paved   ☐ Sand / Grass   ☐ Gravel
☐ Picnic Table   ☐ Fire ring   ☐ Trees   ☐ Lawn
☐ Patio   ☐ Kid Friendly   ☐ Pet Friendly
☐ Store   ☐ Cafe   ☐ Firewood
☐ Ice   ☐ Security   ☐ Quiet   ☐ Noisy

Our Rating: ☆ ☆ ☆ ☆ ☆

GPS: _____

Altitude: _____

Cell Service / Carrier: _____

☐ Antenna Reception   ☐ Satellite TV   ☐ Cable TV
☐ Wifi Available   ☐ Free ☐ Fee $_____

Memberships: _____

Ammenities: _____

Location	☺	☺	☹	Water Pressure	☺	☺	☹
Restrooms	☺	☺	☹	Laundry	☺	☺	☹
Pool	☺	☺	☹	Hot Tub	☺	☺	☹

PLACES VISITED / ACTIVITIES: _____

_____

_____

_____

_____

PEOPLE MET / NEW FRIENDS: _____

_____

_____

_____

_____

FOOD, DINING & RESTAURANTS: _____

_____

_____

_____

_____

HIGHLIGHTS / MEMORABLE EVENTS: _____

_____

_____

_____

_____

PLACES TO GO & THINGS TO DO FOR NEXT TIME: _____

_____

_____

_____

_____

NOTES:

Date: _____	From: _____	Beginning Mileage:
Weather:	To: _____	Ending Mileage:
☀ ⛅ ☂ ❄ 🌡 ❄🌡 🎐 💨	Route Taken: _____ _____	Total Miles Traveled:

CAMPGROUND INFORMATION

Name:_____	Our Rating: ☆ ☆ ☆ ☆ ☆
Address:_____	GPS: _____
Phone:_____	Altitude: _____

Site #_____ $_____ ☐ Day ☐ Week ☐ Month

			Cell Service / Carrier:_____
☐ First Visit	☐ Return Visit	☐ Easy Access	☐ Antenna Reception ☐ Satellite TV ☐ Cable TV
☐ Site Level	☐ Back-in	☐ Pull-through	☐ Wifi Available ☐ Free ☐ Fee $_____
☐ 15 amp	☐ 30 amp	☐ 50 amp	Memberships: _____
☐ Water	☐ Sewer	☐ Shade ☐ Sun	
☐ Paved	☐ Sand / Grass	☐ Gravel	Ammenities:_____
☐ Picnic Table	☐ Fire ring	☐ Trees ☐ Lawn	Location ☺ ☺ ☹ Water Pressure ☺ ☺ ☹
☐ Patio	☐ Kid Friendly	☐ Pet Friendly	Restrooms ☺ ☺ ☹ Laundry ☺ ☺ ☹
☐ Store	☐ Cafe	☐ Firewood	Pool ☺ ☺ ☹ Hot Tub ☺ ☺ ☹
☐ Ice	☐ Security	☐ Quiet ☐ Noisy	

PLACES VISITED / ACTIVITIES: _____
_____
_____
_____

PEOPLE MET / NEW FRIENDS: _____
_____
_____
_____

FOOD, DINING & RESTAURANTS: _____
_____
_____
_____

HIGHLIGHTS / MEMORABLE EVENTS: _____
_____
_____
_____

PLACES TO GO & THINGS TO DO FOR NEXT TIME: _____
_____
_____
_____

NOTES:

Date: _____	From: _____	Beginning Mileage:
Weather:	To: _____	
☀ ⛅ ☂ ❄	Route Taken: _____	Ending Mileage:
🌡 ❄🌡 🎐 ☁	_____	Total Miles Traveled:

CAMPGROUND INFORMATION

Name:_____

Our Rating: ☆ ☆ ☆ ☆ ☆

Address:_____

GPS: _____

Phone:_____

Altitude: _____

Site #_____ $_____ ☐ Day ☐ Week ☐ Month

Cell Service / Carrier:_____

☐ First Visit	☐ Return Visit	☐ Easy Access
☐ Site Level	☐ Back-in	☐ Pull-through
☐ 15 amp	☐ 30 amp	☐ 50 amp
☐ Water	☐ Sewer	☐ Shade ☐ Sun
☐ Paved	☐ Sand / Grass	☐ Gravel
☐ Picnic Table	☐ Fire ring	☐ Trees ☐ Lawn
☐ Patio	☐ Kid Friendly	☐ Pet Friendly
☐ Store	☐ Cafe	☐ Firewood
☐ Ice	☐ Security	☐ Quiet ☐ Noisy

☐ Antenna Reception ☐ Satellite TV ☐ Cable TV
☐ Wifi Available ☐ Free ☐ Fee $_____

Memberships: _____

Ammenities:_____

Location	☺ ☺ ☹	Water Pressure	☺ ☺ ☹
Restrooms	☺ ☺ ☹	Laundry	☺ ☺ ☹
Pool	☺ ☺ ☹	Hot Tub	☺ ☺ ☹

PLACES VISITED / ACTIVITIES: _____
_____
_____
_____

PEOPLE MET / NEW FRIENDS: _____
_____
_____
_____

FOOD, DINING & RESTAURANTS: _____
_____
_____
_____

HIGHLIGHTS / MEMORABLE EVENTS: _____
_____
_____
_____

PLACES TO GO & THINGS TO DO FOR NEXT TIME: _____
_____
_____
_____

NOTES:

Made in the USA
Las Vegas, NV
02 October 2022

56421240R00069